MATTHEW IN HISTORY

MATTHEW IN HISTORY

Interpretation, Influence, and Effects

ULRICH LUZ

FORTRESS PRESS/MINNEAPOLIS

MATTHEW IN HISTORY
Interpretation, Influence, and Effects

Scripture quotations, unless otherwise noted, are from the New Revised Standard Version of the Bible, copyright © 1989 by the Division of Christian Education of the National Council of the Churches of Christ in the United States of America.

Cover design: Patricia Boman
Cover art: Jusepe de Ribera (Spanish, 1591–1652), *Saint Matthew*, 1632, Oil on canvas, 50½ × 38½". Courtesy Kimbell Art Museum, Fort Worth, Texas.

Library of Congress Cataloging-in-Publication Data

Luz, Ulrich.
    Matthew in history / interpretation, influence, and effects / Ulrich Luz.
      p.   cm.
    "A revision of the Sprunt lectures delivered at Union Theological Seminary, Richmond, Virginia in 1990"—Pref.
    Includes bibliographical references and indexes.
    ISBN 0-8006-2833-0 (alk. paper) :
    1. Bible. N.T. Matthew—Historiography. 2. Bible. N.T. Matthew—Criticism, interpretation, etc.—History. 3. Bible. N.T. Matthew—Influence. I. Title.
BS2575.2.L88   1994
226.2'06'09—dc20
                                     94-8912
                                       CIP

Manufactured in the U.S.A.   AF 1-2833

98   97   96   95   94   1   2   3   4   5   6   7   8   9   10

CONTENTS

PREFACE

This book is a revision of the Sprunt Lectures delivered at Union Theological Seminary, Richmond, Virginia, in 1990. I thank the faculty and President T. Hartley Hall IV for having invited me to give these lectures and for the opportunity to become better acquainted with the New World. The lectures were subsequently delivered also at Pittsburgh Theological Seminary and some of them also in other parts of the United States. I am especially grateful to the students for their pertinent questions, which helped me to realize how different the context of American and European students of the Bible is today. I doubt that the ideas articulated in this book could have been formulated without the problems, questions, and suggestions of students, whether at home in Switzerland or in the United States.

This is my first book written originally in English. It is a risk to write in a foreign language, and I am a bit proud to have done it! I would like to thank the publishers for accepting this risk, especially for their assistance with English style. If some formulations still sound strange to American ears, it is not their fault.

ABBREVIATIONS

AB	Anchor Bible
AKG	Arbeiten zur kirchengeschichte
CSEL	Corpus scriptorum ecclesiasticorum latinorum
DS	Denzinger-Schönmetzer, *Enchiridion symbolorum*
EKKNT	Evangelisch-katholischer Kommentar zum Neuen Testament
EvTh	*Evangelische Theologie*
FRLANT	Forschungen zur Religion und Literatur des Alten und Neuen Testaments
GCS	Griechischen christlichen Schriftsteller
HTKNT	Herders theologischer Kommentar zum Neuen Testament
HUT	Hermeneutische Untersuchungen zur Theologie
J.W.	Josephus, *Jewish Wars*, ed. B. Niese, r.p. 1955
KBANT	Kommentare und Beiträge zum Alten und Neuen Testament
NPNF	Nicene and Post-Nicene Fathers
NTS	*New Testament Studies*
PuP	Päpste und Papsttum
QD	Quaestiones disputatae
SC	Sources chrétiennes
SL	Series Latina

TDNT	G. Kittel and G. Friedrich (eds.), *Theological Dictionary of the New Testament*
TRE	*Theologische Realenzyklopädie*
TU	Texte und Untersuchungen
WUNT	Wissenschaftliche Untersuchungen zum Neuen Testament
ZTK	*Zeitschrift für Theologie und Kirche*

INTRODUCTION

These chapters have two roots in my personal and scholarly life. The first root is my experience as teacher of New Testament in Göttingen and Bern for almost twenty years. In our universities the most important New Testament course is the so-called proseminar. This is an intensive course, and its goal is to give beginners their own scholarly competence in exegesis. Here all the different methodological approaches are taught, the classical diachronic ones (text criticism, source criticism, form criticism, social history, history of ideas and religion, and so on) and the newer synchronic methods (such as structural approaches and literary criticism). At the same time the proseminar tries to give to the students some awareness of the hermeneutical relevance of these methods—their possibilities, limits, and biases. A scholarly exegetical paper of twenty to thirty pages is expected from every student as a kind of test for his or her methodological independence. The proseminar is—in my opinion—one of the few excellent pedagogical institutions of German and Swiss exegetical education.

For the teachers, the proseminar is a chance to get to know the students and to learn what they feel and think about their work. My general and continuous impression during the last years has been that they have very few expectations from historical criticism and other scholarly methods. The time of the revolutionary years after 1968 is over; at that time we experienced a general protest against historical method, because it was believed to be bourgeois.

1

For various reasons, however, there remains a skepticism against it. The abundance of scholarly books in the field of New Testament studies is discouraging for our students. It irritates them that the hundreds and thousands of New Testament scholars in the world have such different opinions and that a full consensus is almost impossible. In almost all of the books they read, they find contrary opinions. What is the value of historical criticism when everything is hypothetical and almost nothing is clear? It also irritates them that, on the basis of different theoretical presuppositions, scholars produce entirely different structural analyses of the texts. They have a feeling of helplessness: What competence can *we* have, if even among the savants there is only dispute?

But it is not only this feeling of helplessness vis-à-vis the sophisticated proceedings of scholarly methods that makes students skeptical. They feel that these methods, and particularly the historical-critical explanation of texts, do not really lead to understanding the texts. Quite the contrary, they separate the texts from our experience and life instead of bringing both into a helpful dialogue. My students ask: What does all this have to do with *me?* What do all these explanatory trifles have to do with *my* understanding of the text? They experience two big "ditches" and do not find help to cross them: the ditch between past and present and the ditch between the objective reconstruction of the meaning of a text and its significance for them personally. That is why alternative methods of interpreting the Bible, particularly the depth-psychological approach, are so popular among them. These methods enforce an identification with the text without any reflection about the historical distance. As a New Testament teacher, I am continually confronted with the fundamental feeling of the uneasiness of my students. They force me to ask what it means for *me*—as a concrete person in a concrete situation—to *understand* a text that I have explained with a complicated and elaborate set of methods.

The second root in my life is an entirely different one. When the authors of the new ecumenical commentary Evangelisch-katholischer Kommentar met for the first time, the question of the purpose of the new series of commentaries was raised. We wanted this series to reflect the confessional problem—namely, the relation of the different confessional churches to their common basis, the Bible. It was in this context that the phrase "history of effects" came up. What does it mean? The phrase derives from the German word *Wirkungsgeschichte*—one of those marvelous German words that is almost untranslatable into other languages. We took it over from the philosophical hermeneutic of Hans Georg Gadamer, in his book *Truth and Method*.[1] In the English version of Gadamer's book it is translated as "effective history." It means two things: First, that historical events or books like the Bible are effective; they have an impact on those who live afterward. At the same time, it means the effects—that is, the consequences or impact—of the text on historical events. In this sense we should translate it better with "history of effects." In this way much of church history, and even of our secular history, is part of the "history of effects" of the Bible. Wilhelm Linss translated it as "history of influence"; maybe this is the best translation, because it is the most neutral one.[2] By the concept of *Wirkungsgeschichte* we meant that the future commentary series should try to demonstrate and to analyze the kind of role the biblical texts played in the historical process of the confessional diversification of the churches. We wanted to contribute to an ecumenical spirit by understanding more clearly how other churches became what they are through our common Bible.

At that time we had no idea of what the hermeneutical consequences of this attempt would be. In the first volumes of the new commentary, "history of effects" was presented mainly in appendixes and excursuses that had no function in the commentary proper. But in reality the hermeneutical bearing of the decision to include the history of influence was far-reaching. When we included "history of effects" in our program, we wanted to exclude the possibility of interpreting texts in isolation from the realm of history. But it was also a decision against the purely objectivized history of historical criticism: History is not a reconstructed world with no relation to us, but rather a meaningful memory.[3]

---

1. *Truth and Method*, trans. J. Weisenheimer and D. G. Marshall (New York: Crossroad, 1982).

2. In his translation of the first volume of my commentary, *Matthew 1–7: A Continental Commentary* (Minneapolis: Fortress Press, 1989) 11.

3. The expression is a reminder of A. Heuss, *Verlust der Geschichte* (Göttingen: Vandenhoeck & Ruprecht, 1959). He opposes "history as memory" to "history as science," which is destroying the living history as memory.

\ Verlust

I have worked for about ten years now on my commentary on Matthew. My hermeneutical reflections are a kind of secondary fruit of this work. Studying the history of exegesis and the history of influence of the Matthean texts led me to a strange experience. I found that many of the numerous modern historical-critical commentaries were tedious. Apart from the fact that they tend to repeat time and again the same things, I often had the impression that they did not add much to a real understanding of the texts. More frequently I found myself sympathetic with Karl Barth's famous distinction between the enigma of explaining documents through scholarly exegesis and the "enigma of the substance," which very often escapes these scholarly efforts.[4] But I studied the classical commentaries on the Gospels—those by Origen, Thomas Aquinas, Dionysius Carthusius, John Calvin, Musculus, Juan Maldonado, and Cornelius a Lapide—with enthusiasm. I had the impression that they really *understood* something about the meaning of the texts. The study of the history of interpretation and the history of influence became more and more fascinating for me.

Why do I find the history of influence fascinating? Working historically-critically with Matthew's texts and working on their history of interpretation, I had to reflect about my impressions and fascinations. I had to reflect on what the understanding of texts means and what historical-critical research and the history of exegesis contribute to it. Where does the experience of the hermeneutical sterility of historical-critical work and the distinguishable experience of the productivity of the history of interpretation come from? These chapters are some afterthoughts or side-reflections from my work on the commentary of Matthew. They are also an attempt to respond to some of the feelings and questions of my students. These chapters do not yet present a complete and reflected model of understanding. They are contributions to the development of a hermeneutic.

---

4. In the preface to the second edition of his commentary on Romans: *The Epistle to the Romans*, trans. E. C. Hoskyns (Oxford: Oxford Univ. Press; London: Milford, 1933) 8f.

ONE

THE LIMITS OF THE HISTORICAL-CRITICAL METHOD

The Situation of German New Testament Scholarship

If you read American books about almost any New Testament topic that contain a history of research, you often observe the same thing: German names of the nineteenth century are listed, such as F. C. Baur and H. J. Holtzmann; names of the early twentieth century follow, such as Albert Schweitzer, Adolf Schlatter, Rudolf Bultmann, Martin Dibelius, Günther Bornkamm, and Ernst Käsemann. Then the German names disappear, and the history of research proceeds with English or American names. Implicitly this expresses a conviction: the great era of prominent German New Testament scholarship is over. I partly share this impression. A certain exhaustion and scholasticism strikes me when I look at the situation in Germany.

One reason for this lack of German prominence might be the abundance of commentaries: Many German-speaking New Testament scholars, myself included, do indeed write commentaries. The commentary format is not the best medium to present entirely new approaches; instead it presents and summarizes the state of research, provides surveys, and endeavors to strike a balance. Another reason might be found in the two typically German approaches to the diachronic interpretation of the Gospels in this century, tradition criticism and redaction criticism. They seem to have exhausted their possibilities: Redaction-critical interpretation of the Gospels in its later stage has produced many increasingly detailed monographs and papers, in which hundreds of pages are devoted to explaining jots and tittles of one pericope. Tradition criticism, on the other hand, has produced such a mass of different and contradicting hypotheses that it disillusions both scholars and students.[1]

In spite of this methodological exhaustion, German scholarship has not given up the historical approach. Quite the opposite is true. When I look at how new methodological approaches were developed or received in Germany, I have to say that the more historical the approach, the better chance it had to be received. I think this is the reason why an ahistorical structuralism of the French type never had a chance in Germany. It was busy with "text worlds" that seemed to exist only in the heads of the interpreting professors and apart from history. Therefore only a synchronic approach like rhetorical criticism has a chance to be received here,[2] because its structuring principles are taken from the historical world of antiquity. That historical connection is also the reason why the sociological approach developed by Gerd Theissen was so successful. Theissen always emphasized that he understood his work as historical, as a revision and a better realization of the sociological dimension that was inherent already in traditional form criticism.[3]

Briefly, what we observe in the German-speaking world is a certain exhaustion of historical criticism; but the *principle* of historical interpretation of the biblical texts is as firmly advocated as ever. This is true even for New Testament theology. Theology of the New Testament seems to me the classical expression and the best contribution of Germany to worldwide New Testament scholarship. But recent approaches, such as Leonhard Goppelt's[4] and

---

1. An example: H. Thyen, "Johannesevangelium," *TRE* 18.211, explicitly gives up the diachronic approach to the Fourth Gospel as leading to nothing. He does not advocate simply a structural approach, however, but tries to understand the Gospel as a "verbal part of a concrete situation of communication," i.e., to understand it once again historically.

2. See K. Berger's excellent "Formgeschichte," which is based on rhetorical categories: *Formgeschichte des Neuen Testaments* (Heidelberg: Quelle & Meyer, 1984).

3. See G. Theissen, *Social Reality and the Early Christians*, trans. M. Kohl (Minneapolis: Fortress Press, 1992) 3–8.

4. L. Goppelt, *Theology of the New Testament*, trans. J. Alsup (2 vols.; Grand Rapids, Mich.: Eerdmans, 1981, 1982).

Klaus Berger's[5] theologies, are a mere *history* of New Testament theological ideas. Here again we have an example of the unbroken dominance of historical thinking in the German world. But the question of identifying the theological dignity of a certain piece of the history of theology remains open.

Historical thinking therefore clearly dominates New Testament research in Germany. But its reception and its application to the present become more difficult. Here I see the deepest crisis of our historical thinking. Let me return to the situation among our students. Students and ministers who read our papers and books ask, "What does all this have to do with *my* experiences and with *my* life?" The question sounds simple, but it goes to the heart of the problem. What is the intention of historical-critical research? It is to separate the texts from their present-day reader, to transpose them back into their own time, and to reconstruct their original meaning as intended by their authors or received by their original readers, respectively—in short, to reconstruct the original communication between the author and his first recipients. It tries to reconstruct how and why the text came to be, what it intended, and what its effects were. With this aim, it uses both external data— for example, from archeology or the history of ideas, motives, and language—and intratextual data such as information about the implied readers and the implied author of a text. Historical-critical research uses the later information as a window to the extratextual world, as a kind of mirror in which the outside world is reflected indirectly. The world into which historical-critical method transposes a text is its own world of the past and, by definition, not our world. Already Bultmann deplored the fact that historical-critical philology tended to *use* texts as *sources* in order to reconstruct an image of a past time but that it neglected its proper task and goal: to *understand* texts simply for the sake of understanding.[6]

The historical-critical method does deal with the area of experience, but it is the experience of persons in the past, not ours today. Moreover, the method can *describe*, but it does not show

---

5. K. Berger, *Urchristliche Theologiegeschichte*, forthcoming.
6. R. Bultmann, "The Problem of Hermeneutics," in *Essays Philosophical and Theological*, trans. J. C. G. Greig (London: SCM, 1955) 236ff.

how to *use* the texts today. Søren Kierkegaard once gave a nice example of what the "objectivity" of the "philosophers" means. "It is," he says, "as if you find in a second-hand shop a board on which is written, 'Laundry.' But this board in the second-hand shop is completely irrelevant, because you cannot drop off any clothes to be washed at the second-hand shop."[7] Likewise, the only thing historical-critical method can do is to affirm that the original setting in life of this board was this or that; it cannot determine the proper use of the texts. The historical-critical method is like approaching a cathedral and analyzing its stones—their provenance, their corrosion, their way of being fixed and put one upon another. But you never realize in this way what a cathedral really is. You grasp its beauty only when you enter it, sit down and pray, or listen to the organ.[8] Historical criticism by itself often does not lead to a *productive* distance from the texts, but instead has no relation to it. What if we know what Paul wanted to say to the Corinthians 1,939 years ago? Or what if we know what Jesus wanted to say to the Pharisees and what a tradition about him said to the pre-Markan, the Markan, the Matthean, or the Lukan community? In the latter case, the situation is even more difficult, because we must decide not only about the significance that a text of the past might ultimately have for us, but also whether its meaning for the Pharisees or the pre-Markan or the Markan community is most important for us. The historical-critical method aims at establishing the past meaning as objectively as possible; and at the same time it leaves the decision about its possible significance for today totally up to the subjectivity of every interpreter. It creates a distance between the biblical text of the past and us, but it does not by itself offer the possibility of bringing the text back to us. The scholar in the study, remote from everyday life, may be helped by it, but not the preacher, who has to proclaim the truth today, nor the ordinary Christian, who wants to live as a Christian. Historical criticism also has a tendency to cut the exegete off from the living community,

---

7. S. Kierkegaard, *Either/Or* (Garden City, N.Y.: Doubleday, 1959) 31.
8. See C. Müller, *Exegese und Wirklichkeit* (Ph.D. diss.; Bern, 1987) 166: "And who is able to notice that this building is a cathedral, where in this very moment the Lord's Supper is celebrated?"

as Walter Wink rightly observes;[9] it is a solitary or, in the best case, an elitist enterprise.

Another observation from present-day Germany and Switzerland confirms this impression. While many students read historical-critical books only because they need them for their exams and many pastors no longer read them at all, the voluminous books of the depth psychologist Eugen Drewermann are best-sellers. Among other books, he has written two huge volumes about depth psychology and exegesis.[10] According to Eugen Drewermann, the historical-critical method cannot but accentuate the singularity and relativity of every conviction of faith; in itself it "cannot lead to a theological insight into the *lasting* significance of the text."[11] Drewermann's general assumption is that the biblical texts are symbolizations of the divine truths that constitute the depth of the human soul and that all historical particularities and specific historical circumstances have to be ignored in order to detect the lasting truth of the texts. Historical-critical exegesis, according to him, prevents the text from becoming an event in the life of the reader. I cannot give a detailed discussion of Drewermann's hermeneutic here, but I want to say that his books, in spite of many points where I disagree, probably are the most exciting event in the field of hermeneutics in the last decade. They really challenge an exegesis that, as Berger says, has rendered our religious experiences homeless.[12] The reason for Drewermann's success is that he helps the readers to see how the biblical texts speak to *them* and can have an impact on their lives.

Let me summarize. I can do it with the words of Jürgen Moltmann: "The more historical consciousness reiterates what Paul said as a child of his time to his contemporaries, the more the present time gets rid of his claims."[13] And Hans Georg Gadamer says: "The

9. W. Wink, *The Bible in Human Transformation* (Philadelphia: Fortress Press, 1973) 10–12.

10. E. Drewermann, *Tiefenpsychologie und Exegese* (2 vols.; Olten: Walter, 1984, 1985). See also his *Das Markusevangelium* (2 vols.; Olten: Walter, 1987, 1988). A commentary on the Gospel of Matthew is forthcoming.

11. Drewermann, *Tiefenpsychologie und Exegese*, 1.24.

12. K. Berger, *Hermeneutik des Neuen Testaments* (Gütersloh: G. Mohn, 1988) 132.

13. J. Moltmann, *Perspectiven der Theologie* (Munich: Kaiser, 1968) 115.

text that is understood historically is forced to abandon its claim that it is offering something true. We think we understand when we see the past from the historical standpoint . . . and seek to reconstruct the historical horizon. In fact, however, we have given up the claim to find in the past any truth valid and intelligible to ourselves."[14]

The Relative Insignificance of Historical Meaning

Why does the reconstruction of the original situation and of the original meaning of a biblical text have so little significance for us, in spite of the fact that it was so important for many generations before us, especially in the eighteenth and nineteenth centuries? It is not that history had a fundamental importance for the thinkers of the Enlightenment. In his famous dictum in his tractate to Schumann, G. E. Lessing said that the "accidental truths of history can never become the proof of necessary truths of reason" and that "nothing can be proved through historical truths."[15] "Belief in historical narratives of any kind whatsoever," says Spinoza, "cannot afford us the knowledge and love of God" but is of pedagogical value only.[16] The question of the meaning of past texts and the question of their truth are two entirely different questions for him.[17] For Immanuel Kant, the Bible and exegesis are pillars of the statutory ecclesiastical faith and authority for those not yet of age mentally. Pure religion does not depend on them.[18] In other words, the exegesis influenced by the basic ideas of the Enlightenment separates the (historical) question of the meaning of a text from the (fundamental) question of its truth. The two questions have nothing to do with one another.

14. H. G. Gadamer, *Truth and Method*, trans. J. Weisenheimer and D. G. Marshall (New York: Crossroad, 1982) 270.

15. G. E. Lessing, "On the Proof of the Spirit and of Power," in *Lessing's Theological Writings*, trans. H. Chadwick (London: A. C. Black, 1956) 53.

16. B. Spinoza, *Tractatus theologico-politicus*, trans. S. Shirley (Leiden: Brill, 1989) 104f.

17. See H. Frei, *The Eclipse of Biblical Narrative* (London and New Haven, Conn.: Yale University Press, 1974) 42f.

18. I. Kant, *Religion within the Limits of Reason Alone*, trans. Th. M. Greene and H. Hudson (Chicago and London: Open Court Company, 1934) 97f.

But what kind of positive significance did the historical question have for the exegetes after the Enlightenment? Their interest in history and in the original meaning of the biblical text could not have been to find in them real, eternal truth, because this is a question not of history but of reason. The history testified by the Bible can provide examples and models for this truth in the best case; but the eternal truth of reason does not depend on them. Therefore the interest in history on the part of Enlightenment scholars and their successors in the nineteenth century was primarily a negative one: the history of the Bible turned out to be mere human history and not a basis for eternal truth. It could not be the basis of dogma. Critically it helped toward the abolition of authoritative and heteronomous norms of the church. For this abolition it was not even necessary that the original meaning of biblical texts contradicted ecclesiastical dogmas and norms. The thoroughly human character of the Bible and of the history behind it already made it an impossible foundation for eternal truth. History could not be the basis of any truth. Historical-critical exegesis, as a child of the literary exegesis of the Reformation, does not question the relation between historical description and truth, but only "the coincidence of the description with how the facts really occurred."[19] Historical-critical research therefore only had an emancipative character and helped contribute to the autonomy of the rational human subject, but it could not help establish the fundamental theological question of truth. This is—I think—the basic problem of historical-critical exegesis, the results of which today can be seen in its theological and existential insignificance.

The historical-critical method today has lost even this emancipative character, and that is the final reason why it has become meaningless for us. From what should we become emancipated? In modern Western Protestantism, Christian doctrines, dogmas, and norms lost their binding character a long time ago. They remain, if they remain at all, the basis of personal individual convictions. In Protestant churches, at least in Switzerland, the only dogma seems to be that every Christian—and particularly every pastor— can believe what he or she wants, as long as she or he respects

19. Frei, *Eclipse*, 8.

the plurality of the church and shows a certain vague respectfulness of its tradition. In the Roman Catholic church it is different; but for Catholics, the Christian truth never depended on the results of exegesis, and therefore the emancipative power of historical criticism always was a more limited one.

Today, by contrast, the confidence in the strength of reason and in the qualities of autonomous human subjects has rapidly decreased, at least in Europe. After two World Wars, in the midst of still tremendous amounts of atomic and chemical weapons, we face the destruction of our natural resources and the unequal distribution of economic wealth at home and in the Third World. We are afraid of the possibilities of high technology and computerization exerting control over human life in the hands of technocrats. Realizing all this, we have little trust in the power of human reason and the autonomy of human subjects. The situation of intellectuals and many other people in Europe, at least in Germany and Switzerland, is comparable with that of many parts of the Hellenistic world after the breakdown of the classical Greek polis-system. It is characterized by pessimism, distrust of reason, new age visions, withdrawal from the political to the individual world, a longing for lasting values and authority, and susceptibility to various kinds of religions and superstitions. We are in a situation in which many people *want* someone or something, a God or a divine word, to touch them and give them authority or clear direction in life and to provide them with a hope that transcends this hopeless world. In this situation the historical-critical interpretation of the Bible, which is inherently incapable of making contact with the eternal, because it leads only to temporal and historical interpretations of it, has become rather meaningless. Here I find the deepest reason for the hermeneutical crisis that we observe today.

I now want to ask about the concepts of understanding that are implicit in the biblical texts. These, of course, are not immediately authoritative for our hermeneutics. That would be a kind of hermeneutical biblicism or a new form of sacred hermeneutics. I think that different genres must be understood differently, for instance, a newspaper, a poem, a liturgical text, a novel, a prayer, a letter, or a Gospel story. Every text implicitly contains the idea of how it wants to be understood. Therefore the hermeneutical implications of the biblical texts should be questioned and then interrelated with our own concepts and ideas. Hermeneutics of the biblical texts cannot be developed except in dialogue with the biblical texts.[20] Regarding the biblical texts, two points are particularly important for me, the holistic character and the productive power of biblical texts.

The Holistic Character of the Understanding of Biblical Texts

What does it mean to understand a biblical text? Biblical texts are always secondary to biblical history and to the life of the people of Israel or the early Christian communities. The written biblical texts are something like conserved or frozen life, like a piece of frozen food that can be preserved and transported. But, like frozen food, they cannot be eaten as long as they remain frozen. Or they are like a photograph, a picture of a moment of life; as a photograph it is lifeless, and the figures no longer move or laugh. Biblical texts as texts are secondary effects of life. Understanding them means to restore them back to life. Historical reconstruction means to describe the life situations to which the texts—as their frozen memories—belonged and to which they referred. But again, this is not yet to understand the texts. Frozen food becomes meaningful only when it is unfrozen and can be eaten. A photograph becomes meaningful only when it is combined with our memory and when, through it, the persons represented in it come alive again in our hearts. In a similar way biblical texts are meaningful only when they become part of our life. In other words, to understand a New Testament text does not mean to understand the words of the text

---

20. See H. Weder, *Neutestamentliche Hermeneutik* (Zürich: Theologischer Verlag Zürich, 1986). Weder's hermeneutic comes very close to a New Testament theology; the context of the modern readers of the Bible does not have equal weight with the biblical texts. This is different from the hermeneutic of K. Berger (*Hermeneutik*). For him the analysis of the situation is the point of departure; the biblical texts, however, do have a fundamental significance for his hermeneutical model too—particularly stories and parables—although they cannot be directly authoritative but provide *models* for application.

only but to understand the living Christ to whom it testifies and the life situation that was shaped by him, and to understand both as a gift, a question, and a challenge for our own lives. Understanding such texts is not an intellectual knowledge that can be separated from other dimensions of life; rather this understanding is possible only when it encompasses human life in its totality—intellectual insights, feelings, actions, and suffering.

I take the parables as the first example. Understanding the parable of the workers in the vineyard means not simply to *know* that God is a "generous employer" but to *rejoice* about this (Matt. 20:15) and to share the happiness of co-workers who were overpaid. The story of the good Samaritan is understood only when the Jewish listeners' own attitudes toward Samaritans are changed through it, because they realize that God does not evaluate priests, Levites, and Samaritans in the same way as they would have (Luke 10:30-35). Many, if not most, of the parables of Jesus are understood only when a change in the life of the readers or listeners takes place.

A second example is the Gospel of Mark: Peter understood who Jesus was, namely, the Christ (Mark 8:27-30). Yet he understood nothing, because he was going to protest against the suffering of the Son of man and against his own suffering in discipleship (Mark 8:31-34). The misunderstanding of the disciples in the Gospel of Mark comes to its peak only after the disciples have understood intellectually who Jesus is, namely, the Christ. A full understanding involves discipleship with Christ.

A third example is Matthew's hermeneutics. The parable of the four soils (Matt. 13:3-23) is an interesting text. Matthew distinguishes among "hearing," "understanding," and "bearing fruit" (vv. 18-23). Understanding has an intellectual character, and it happens through Jesus' ongoing teaching of the disciples (cf. 13:18-23, 36-52; 15:15-20).[21] Yet the only listener in this parable about whom Matthew explicitly says that he or she understands is the one who brings fruit—thirty, sixty, and one-hundredfold (13:23). For Matthew, fruitless understanding is impossible and leads to the final condemnation by the judge of the world, as the end of the Sermon

---

21. See U. Luz, *Das Evangelium nach Matthäus II (Mt 8–17)* (EKKNT I/2; Neu-kirchen-Vluyn: Neukirchener; Zürich: Benziger, 1990) 318.

on the Mount shows; those who say "Lord, Lord" have understood who Jesus is, and they address him in a dogmatically correct manner. But this does not help them (7:21-23).

A fourth example is Paul's polemic against the different factions in the church of Corinth. His position is that any Christian wisdom that divides Christ and absolutizes human theological positions contradicts the word of the cross. Love is the criterion of true Christian knowledge (1 Cor. 1:18—3:4). No real wisdom, no understanding of the cross, is possible without love. Consider finally the Johannine concept of knowledge (*ginōskein*), in which understanding transcends the intellectual realm, points to existence in communion with God and Christ, and is ultimately identical with faith and love.[22]

With this discussion we are far removed from modern scientific understanding. Nothing is more different from what the *Gospels* intend to convey than to write a scholarly historical commentary or a literary-critical analysis. From the point of view of the Gospels, it is impossible to set the interpreter at a distance from the text and to interpret it in its own world, different from the world of the interpreter. It is also impossible to interpret the text *alone*, leaving the window to the real world—of the past and present—closed. From the point of view of the biblical text, the interpretation of the text and the interpretation of the life of the interpreter—the past and the present—must always remain together. Only when the life of the interpreter and his or her situation comes into a new light through the text is the text understood and brought to new life.[23] Understanding is an "event," as Ernst Fuchs taught us,[24] not a product of intellectual activity. Therefore it is an open question whether we historical-critical exegetes, whose task it is to promote the *explanation* of the text, are really able to promote an

22. R. Bultmann, *ginōskō*, TDNT 1.711–13.
23. See C. Boff, *Theology and Praxis*, trans. R. Barr (Maryknoll, N.Y.: Orbis, 1987) 151: To understand the Scriptures means to understand the present according to the Scriptures.
24. See E. Fuchs, *Marburger Hermeneutik* (HUT 9; Tübingen: Mohr-Siebeck, 1968) 19: "Understanding . . . causes us . . . to move." In this section of his book, Fuchs differentiates between explaining and understanding, modifying Dilthey's concept.

understanding of the text through our explanations. I leave the question open for the moment; it should not be pushed aside by a quick intellectual answer.

José Míguez Bonino, in his brilliant comments on hermeneutics in *Doing Theology in a Revolutionary Situation*, objects to Western thinking that "truth" belongs to "a universe complete in itself," which is first understood theoretically like an "abstract heaven of truth," and then, only afterward, applied in a concrete historical situation.[25] This Western thinking corresponds not only to the basic idea of a supernatural intellectual cognition of God through revelation but also to the basic ideas of Spinoza and Kant, that the truth of reason is eternal and that history at best offers temporal models or examples of this eternal truth. It corresponds also to the basic Western idea that Christian identity is established by a doctrine, and that ethics does not ultimately touch the essence of Christianity. Míguel Bonino's own claim is that truth does not exist apart from its historical concreteness. This means that theory and praxis, dogmatics and ethics, understanding and application cannot be separated. This basic hermeneutical insight of liberation theology seems very close to the Bible.

What are the consequences? There is no "meaning" of biblical texts that exists for itself, detachable from life and history. Hermeneutically this means that application is not something additional, which can be added afterward to understanding, but, as Gadamer says, is an "integral element of all understanding."[26] Consequently interpretation of the Bible is not only and perhaps not even mainly words, that is, exegesis, dogmatics, preaching, but is also the life of the church and its members "in doing and suffering, . . . in ritual and prayer, in theological work and in personal decisions, in Church organization and ecclesiastical polities . . . , in

---

25. J. Míguez Bonino, *Doing Theology in a Revolutionary Situation* (Philadelphia: Fortress Press, 1975) 88.

26. Gadamer, *Truth and Method*, 275. K. Berger, influenced by P. Ricoeur, proposes another model. He rejects a separation between explaining and understanding and pleads for "the unity of the cognitive capacities" of human beings (*Hermeneutik*, 147), but he separates understanding and application (108ff.). The latter is a "risk" at the interpreter's own responsibility (120). The difficulty of this model is that it tends to separate the receptive attitude of understanding (on the historical level) from the active action of application (on the present-day level); thus, it reduces application to an activity.

wars of religion, and in works of compassionate love." Gerhard Ebeling, whom I quote, understands in his programmatic paper "the history of the church" as "the history of interpretation of Holy Scripture."[27] Or, conversely: The biblical texts do not stimulate so much a "history of (verbal) interpretation" as a history of "fruits" or a "history of effects." In this history whether and how they are understood become apparent. The holistic character of the act of understanding biblical texts forces the historian to look beyond the mere history of exegesis to the history of the church (in the widest sense of the word), because there the biblical texts were understood and applied.

The Power and Productivity of Biblical Texts

The second point is that biblical texts do not *have* a meaning, but rather they *produce* a meaning—new meanings—again and again in history.[28] Historical criticism seems to look in the opposite direction when it asks for the *original* meaning of a biblical text. This search for the original meaning of a text is fundamental to Protestantism: the Renaissance and humanist desire to go "back to the sources" and the Reformation principle "Scripture alone," with its antithesis against later traditions of the church, converge at this point. In the biblical tradition, however, interpretation of old stories and texts did not mean that they were exegeted but rather that they were retold and actualized in new situations. The basic history of Israel had to be told anew, from the Yahwist to the priestly document to Pseudo-Philo and Josephus. With the stories about Jesus the same thing happened in the different Gospels. Jewish legal tradition, from the beginning up to the Temple Scroll and the book of Jubilees, did not so much interpret the Torah as rewrite it.

27. G. Ebeling, "Church History Is the History of the Exposition of Scripture," in idem, *The Word of God and Tradition*, trans. S. H. Hooke (London: Collins, 1968) 28, 26.

28. I understand "meaning" (French *sens*) and "significance" in the way P. Ricoeur understood these terms: To understand the "meaning" of a text is to understand its own intentions; to understand its "significance" is to actualize its meaning in one's own existence ("Preface to Bultmann," in idem, *Essays on Biblical Interpretation* [Philadelphia: Fortress Press, 1980] 67f.).

To an even greater extent, Jesus' interpretation of the Mosaic Torah reveals this freedom. The words of the "Master Prophet" Jesus were not simply repeated and preserved by his prophet-pupils but actualized and enlarged.[29] In Judaism and Christianity from the second century on, texts were interpreted instead of rewritten. This new procedure was a considerable transformation of both Judaism and Christianity and came as a result of the canonization of the texts. Now the text as text, had a dignity beyond its actualizations and new versions. This new understanding did not mean, however, that something like its original meaning was thought to be normative for later times.

Where does this freedom for new interpretations and even new texts come from? Several factors contribute to it. Let me first mention three linguistic points: (1) Every text uses traditional images, models of thought, and concepts. A single author of a text never exhausts all the traditional dimensions of meaning but chooses among the potential meanings of language and motives offered in the tradition. In the transmission of the written text they remain present and enable new choices and accents. (2) Written texts generally tend to be mere shells of words with a rather open meaning, because their author, who could determine their meaning, is no longer present. Therefore transmitted written texts are open to reinterpretation by new recipients in new communication situations.[30] (3) Beyond that, every text has its "blanks," as Wolfgang Iser has shown,[31] a few or many, depending on the genre of the text, that invite the reader to fill them out and bring his or her own world into them.

I may add two theological reasons especially applicable to biblical texts. (4) The biblical texts, like other fundamental religious

29. M. Sato, *Q und Prophetie* (WUNT II/29; Tübingen: Mohr-Siebeck, 1988) 371–406 (a work in critical opposition to the position of the Scandinavian school).

30. P. Ricoeur, "La fonction herméneutique de la distanciation," in F. Bovon and G. Rouiller, eds., *Exegesis. Problèmes de méthode et exercices de lecture* (Neuchâtel and Paris: Delachaux & Niéstlé, 1975) 203ff; J. S. Croatto, *Biblical Hermeneutics*, trans. R. Barr (Maryknoll, N.Y.: Orbis, 1987).

31. W. Iser, *The Act of Reading* (London: Routledge & Kegan Paul, 1978) 182–203. Naturally, the whole approach proposed in this book has many affinities with reader-response criticism. It is in some way a reader-oriented way of understanding and taking seriously the dimension of our past.

texts, proclaim a God who is the Lord of heaven and earth. Therefore they claim an authority that transcends a limited historical situation. They proclaim the living God, who goes "with" the people through history and who reveals again and again that "I am who I will be" (Exod. 3:14). This God is faithful to himself but also creates a new history with the people. (5) Finally, many New Testament texts have something to do with freedom and love, which cannot be prescribed and determined in advance but must be invented anew: New Testament ethical texts are not norms in a formal and legal sense; they give directions and perspectives and invite change and adaptation in new situations.

Therefore biblical texts do not have a simple fixed meaning, which would be identical with their original meaning; they have *power* (cf. Rom. 1:16; 1 Cor. 1:18) to create new meanings for and with new people in new situations. Their meaning cannot be defined simply by scholarly reconstructions, as if they were something like a territory whose borders are to be defined. Interpreting most biblical texts means not *re*production but *production* of meaning out of the transmitted wordshells and with the help of the power of the text.[32] The church fathers and the Reformers spoke at this point about the Holy Spirit. The meaning of a biblical text (and of many literary texts) is a "potential" of meaning.[33] With this I do not mean an idealistic plenitude of meaning, which would be hidden behind the text right from the beginning and would become only partly visible in every historical situation. A biblical text is not a reservoir or a cistern, with a fixed amount of water in it that can be clearly measured. Rather it resembles a source, where new water emerges from the same place. This means that the history of interpretation and effects that a text creates is nothing alien to the text itself, as if the text with its meaning existed at the beginning and then only afterward and secondarily had consequences and created a history of interpretation. The church historian Alfred Schindler once said,

---

32. Boff, *Theology and Praxis*, 153, speaks about "creative remembering" and "productive lecture."

33. H. R. Jauss, *Literaturgeschichte als Provokation* (Frankfurt: Suhrkamp, 1970) 186, speaks about a "potential of meanings" of a literary oeuvre, which is "actualized in the historical process of reception" and equals the "judgment of the centuries" about it.

"The many-voiced echo of centuries . . . belongs to the Bible as a part of itself."[34] Gadamer says that a biblical text "must be understood at every moment, in every particular situation, in a new and different way."[35] The biblical writings are not objects to be investigated, but rather companions on the path of humanity to new lands through the centuries. They are companions that make possible a way to new lands. Following Míguez Bonino we can say that a biblical text does not have a meaning beyond a concrete situation—for example, an idea or an eternal truth—but only a meaning in a concrete situation, where people identify with or protest against the text. Naturally there is a continuity in the story of actualizations and reinterpretations, because it is always the same text that is the point of departure (and the church decided already quite early that this point of departure should not be altered!). And it is the same history to which the texts refer (although memorized and actualized differently in the heart and life of different people). But interpretation must contain also an element of newness, because the text has an "excess of potential meaning over its use" that can live anew in different structures,[36] that is, because texts have potential to create a history. That is why synchronic and structuralist interpretations, insofar as they exclude history, cannot finally understand them. That is also why historical-critical exegesis cannot finally understand them, because it is preoccupied only with the past and cuts the texts off from their power. I would propose to understand the meaning of a biblical text as an interaction of a "kernel of meaning," which corresponds to the given structures of a text, and a "directional meaning," which gives a present direction to the readers on their way to new lands.[37] This is how I would like to do justice to the dynamics of the text.

The model of a "kernel of meaning" and a "directional meaning" implies that the meaning of a text contains an element of

---

34. A. Schindler, "Vom Nutzen und Nachteil der Kirchengeschichte für das Verständnis der Bibel heute," *Reformatio* 30 (1981) 265.
35. Gadamer, *Truth and Method*, 275.
36. P. Ricoeur, "Structure and Hermeneutics," in *The Conflict of Interpretations* (Evanston, Ill.: Northwestern Univ. Press, 1974) 48.
37. See U. Luz, "Erwägungen zur sachgemässen Interpretation neutestamentlicher Texte," *EvTh* 42 (1982) 504.

openness, that it leaves room for changing interpretations. Historical-critical exegesis leaves little room for such an openness, because its aim is to define as precisely as possible *the*—one and definable—original meaning of a text in its original communication situation. Historical-critical interpretation seems to presuppose that each text has *one* meaning, which can be detected through critical analysis and must be described as precisely as possible through scholarly discussion.[38]

Recent reader-response approaches demonstrate new awareness of the openness of texts and the possibility of multiple readings. However, there is an astonishing analogy in the classical hermeneutics of the church: allegorical interpretation never asked for *the* (only) correct interpretation of a text. It always had several different aspects. In the early Middle Ages these aspects were systematized into the doctrine of the fourfold meaning of Scriptures—the literal meaning, which describes the events; the allegorical or mystical meaning, which speaks about the doctrinal truths and the history of salvation; the moral or tropological meaning, with the ethical application for every believer; and the anagogical meaning, which is concerned about eschatology, judgment, and eternal life. This fourfold meaning of Scripture seems to be important for us, because it corresponds to modern insights into the openness of texts and their "blanks," which are to be filled in by the readers,[39] but it also corresponds to the biblical texts themselves.

Let me give an example. The sayings about the tearing out of the right eye and the cutting off of the right hand (Matt. 5:29-30) were interpreted in the church in different ways. For example, the evil eye or hand could mean evil desire, evil thoughts, or evil friends.[40] Naturally this is exegetically wrong. On the other hand, biblical metaphors like "eye" or "hand" are open to new applications. They invite the listeners to combine their own situation with the metaphors and to concretize the "potential freedom" of the

38. Is that a secularized heritage of the Reformation idea of *claritas Scripturae,* which presupposes that each verse of Scripture has *one* meaning only that is usually recognizable without any major difficulties?

39. See Iser, *Act of Reading.*

40. U. Luz, *Matthew 1–7: A Continental Commentary,* trans. W. Linss (Minneapolis: Fortress Press, 1989) 298.

texts. Remarkably, the different allegorical interpretations usually stand one beside the other in the old commentaries and are not mutually exclusive. One and the same text has different possibilities of application expressed by the different allegories. This sounds very modern, but is somewhat contrary to our quest for *the* original meaning. It is strangely at odds with the way that I learned exegesis, where the objective seemed to be to distinguish the correct interpretation of a text from the wrong interpretation.

The partial openness of the meaning of biblical texts and the fact that their meaning has changed in the course of history correspond with each other. From this observation it follows that interpreting biblical texts includes understanding their openness, and detecting their significance for the present is to make use of the freedom they give. Both the given meaning of a text and its potential of freedom are essential for understanding its significance today. The question whether it is possible to distinguish between true and false interpretations of a biblical text remains open.

TWO

HISTORY OF EFFECTS:
A NEW DIMENSION
OF UNDERSTANDING

The History of Effects and Biblical Texts

Biblical texts and the history of effects are related in two ways. On the one hand, they themselves are a result of a history of effects, namely, the effects of the fundamental history of Israel and its later interpretations and also of the fundamental history of Jesus and its earliest textual interpretations. In this way the Gospel according to Matthew is a result of the history of effects of the Gospel according to Mark, the Sayings Source, other Jesus-traditions, and indirectly the history of Jesus itself. On the other hand, the biblical texts have a history of effects, namely, the history of the churches and their confessions after them and, through them, the history of the whole Christian world.

Let me turn to the first aspect. The biblical texts themselves are the result of a history of effects because they are not the ultimate point of departure nor the ultimate authority but products of human reception, human experiences, and human history. The texts of the Gospels themselves are the effect of a historical process, namely, the history of Jesus. They are human responses to and applications of the claim of Jesus. Thus the conception of "history of effects" reminds us of the human, historical, secondary character of our texts. It has an antifundamentalistic impact.

The history of effects reminds us also of the fundamental character of the historical-critical quest for the explanation of biblical texts. Gospel texts are testimonies of the creative power of the transmitted history of Jesus in new situations. They reflect a historical process. Historical-critical interpretation means to reconstruct the way the texts came to be, what they wanted to effect, and what they did effect. Historical-critical interpretation means to retell the story of the origin, the genesis, the intention, and, if possible, the immediate effects of the texts. In this story, both the author and the readers are implied. In other words, historical-critical interpretation explains the texts by giving them back to the life they had in their original setting. It is necessary that sociological and psychological dimensions play an important role already in historical work, because they are part of the life setting from which the texts come, which they reflect, and which they were intended to influence.

Negatively this means that synchronic examination of the text, a structuralist one, or one that uses new literary-critical methods that do not look "through the window" into the real world of the author and his readers or is of limited value for understanding the biblical texts. It is naturally the first *methodological* step of any explanation, because only the text—not the author and the readers nor the situation—is given to us directly. But because the texts come from life, witness to life, and want to produce life, synchronic interpretation of the biblical texts, it seems to me, is only a preliminary step in interpretation. Only historical interpretation, which "looks through the windows" and takes into account the diachronic dimension and the life behind the text, can approach an adequate interpretation of the texts.

More important for the argument in this book is the second aspect, namely, that the biblical texts *have* a history of effects, which is the history between them and us. This history of effects, as we have seen, cannot be separated from the texts, because it is an expression of the texts' own power. It belongs to the texts in the same way that a river flowing away from its source belongs to the source. What is the hermeneutical significance of this history of effects for us? I think it can function as a bridge between the biblical texts and us. The history of effects thus makes it clear that the Bible and we are not separated from one another. I intend this to point beyond the objective truth that all historical events are interrelated.

I am thinking of the more fundamental fact that we too are part of that river that is nourished by the biblical texts. We, the present readers, are not independent from the history of effects of the Bible. Hans Georg Gadamer correctly points out that history is not something distant that we simply analyze but an essential component of life to which we *owe* our language, our way of thinking, our questions, our answers, the whole of our life. Thus biblical texts are not just an object to analyze neutrally. They marked our life and our culture long before we started to analyze them. "Historical objectivism," he says, "conceals the involvement of the historical consciousness itself in effective history."[1] We are indebted to history even when we have to protest against it and to fight against its burden. History is like a river, and we are in a boat carried by that river. Naturally we can analyze the water of this river chemically in different places of the river during our journey in the boat. We can examine its composition, its minerals, its pollution, and so on. But in the meantime we are carried and driven forward by the river, now to this side, now to the other. We owe to the river that transports us our capacity even to make such an analysis and also our capacity to steer our boat. Whatever we say about the biblical texts presupposes that we already have a relationship with them—directly, because we already know, love, or hate them; or indirectly, because we take part in a culture dominated by Christianity and speak a language formed by the Bible. We too are a product of the effective history of the Bible. Gadamer's whole effort is to unmask and overcome the absolutized subject of modern times, which lives as if it would be the ultimate source of all knowledge and deeds. For him, tradition is something like water for a fish, which makes its life possible. If we neglect that and lose the attitude of deep respect for what is a basic element of our life, then we cannot understand texts that are fundamental to us, particularly biblical texts. History of effects brings together the texts and us, their interpreters; or better: the history of effects shows us that we are already together and that it is an illusion to treat the texts in a position of distance and in a merely "objective" way.

1. H. G. Gadamer, *Truth and Method*, trans. J. Weisenheimer and D. G. Marshall (New York: Crossroad, 1982) 268.

After these general remarks I can indicate what were for me the principal hermeneutical gains of the idea of effective history and of the study of the history of effects. I will take my examples from my work on Matthew.

Why and How Interpretations Must Change

The history of influence *describes* the ditch between past and present and makes clear that there was never an interpretation of a text that did not bear the mark of the historical situation of its interpreter. Interpretations change because situations and interpreters change. *There is no uniquely true interpretation of a text.* When the study of the history of effects reveals this fact, it frees our own present from dictates of the biblical past. The understanding of a text even today means something different for different people in different situations, for example, men and women, workers and professors, Africans, Americans, and Europeans. The attempt to understand a biblical text always includes a stable element, namely, the text itself, and a variable element, namely, the interpreter and his or her situation. This view is not to be lamented but seen as necessary for understanding. Because it emphasizes the necessity of introducing this variable element into the process of understanding, the history of influence again has an antifundamentalistic tendency; fundamentalism claims to possess *the* interpretation of an inspired text.

Let me give some examples. The rejection of violence in Matt. 5:38-42 was interpreted literally in pre-Constantinian times: the Christians, obligated to confront the world with the testimony of the gospel, could not participate in worldly affairs, to which wars and armies belonged. Renunciation of military service was therefore part of the missionary testimony of a minority church to a godless world.[2] After Constantine, the Christians too had a responsibility for war and peace. Already Celsus asked bitterly whether Christians, by aloofness from society, wanted to increase the political

---

2. U. Luz, *Matthew 1–7: A Continental Commentary*, trans., W. Linss (Minneapolis: Fortress Press, 1989) 331 nn. 46–49.

power of wild and lawless barbarians.[3] His question constituted a new actuality; from now on, Christians and churches had to choose between the testimony of the gospel, which included renunciation of violence, and responsible participation in political power, which was understood as an act of love toward the world. When they opted for the second possibility, they started to interpret the text within a new framework and in a new way. Augustine's famous *Epistle to Marcellinus* (*Ep* 138) is the most influential example of this new type of interpretation. As we know, the Anabaptists in the time of the Reformation chose the first, the main churches of the Reformation, guided by Augustine, the second possibility.[4] Today the alternative is still the same, except that the participation of Christians in armies and other violent actions of the state has become much more dangerous and murderous. The history of influence of the Bible cannot prescribe a decision in such cases. But it can help us to see the difference between the situations and thus to prevent premature theological condemnations of other Christians' decisions.

A different example is the story of the Canaanite woman (Matt. 15:21-28). It was seen according to a history of salvation model in allegorical interpretation from the fourth until the eighteenth century. The Canaanite woman, according to Hilary,[5] is a proselyte who intercedes for her child, the pagans. They are saved through the Word of Christ alone, without a direct encounter with him. The dogs in the metaphor (v. 26) are the pagans; the children, the Israelites; the bread is the doctrine of the gospel; the table is the Holy Scriptures.[6] This interpretation was repeated again and again for centuries without any change. But the situation changed. The church, in Matthew's time a Jewish-Christian minority group breaking down old borders, became a successful rival of the synagogue and finally triumphed over it and suppressed it. The text,

---

3. Origen, *Contra Celsum* 8.68.
4. See W. Lienemann, *Gewalt und Gewaltverzicht* (Forschungen und Berichte: Forschungsstëlle der Evangelischen Studien-Gemeinschaft 36; Munich: Kaiser, 1982) 182–87.
5. In *Comm. on Matt.* 15:3 = SC 258.36.
6. See Luz, *Das Evangelium nach Matthäus II (Mt 8–17)* (EKKNT I/2; Neukirchen-Vluyn: Neukirchener; Zürich: Benziger, 1990) 430.

originally a promise to a "little flock," gradually became an expression of self-confirmation of a powerful church with a negative impact on those who now were the small minority group, namely, the Jews. The interpretation remained verbally the same, but the situation changed. In this case it was the changed situation that transformed the interpretation into the opposite of what it was originally meant to be.

Interpretations depend on situations and interpreters and must change with them. We cannot simply take over past interpretations, but must create our own. In this respect, our study of the history of influence has an emancipative function and prevents us from becoming mere recipients of the biblical past.

The Location of the Interpreter

One of the basic claims of historical criticism is that by putting distance between a text and us, something of our own bias and prejudices becomes visible. Historical-critical reconstruction is supposed to contribute to a better understanding of the texts *and* of ourselves, the latter indirectly, through realizing how and why we have misunderstood a text before the exegesis. In practice, historical-critical exegesis functions differently. When we work text-critically, structurally, sociologically, and so on, we try to exclude all personal questions, emotions, and prior understandings, but we seldom reflect about what we have excluded. Already Bultmann commented, "It is of no value to *eliminate* the prior understanding: on the contrary, it is to be brought into our consciousness."[7] At this point the study of the history of influence is important in showing how our texts were interpreted, misinterpreted, or neglected by specific interpreters or communities. It thereby reveals our confessional or cultural bias in the process of interpretation. It thus indirectly shows us who and where we are. It helps reintroduce the subject of interpretation into the process of understanding. It has a function similar to that on the personal level of the painting

---

7. R. Bultmann, "The Problem of Hermeneutics," in *Essays Philosophical and Theological*, trans. J. C. G. Grieg (London: SCM, 1955) 253f.

of biblical stories or a dramatic play in a bibliodrama. For this, naturally, the history of influence of a biblical text in the interpreter's own ecclesiastical or cultural tradition is most important. Let me give two examples. It is astonishing how consistently the exegesis of Matt. 6:25-34, the text of the birds and the lilies, overlooks the problem of labor. Almost everybody agrees that this text intends to free us from worry and concern, but not from labor and work. From the time of Augustine[8] and Jerome the fundamental principle derived from this text was, "Work is to be carried out, worry to be removed."[9] We live in a tradition that internalized this text, thinking that it deals with our inner disposition, our inner relation to the world and worldly affairs. Later exegetes, particularly in the Calvinistic tradition, interpreted verse 34, "Do not be concerned about tomorrow," as permission or even a command to be concerned for today and inquired about the kinds of concerns for today that are allowed or necessary.[10] In this way the text was often used to solicit the proper concern for one's livelihood. Exegetically this interpretation is very doubtful. Why does Jesus say that birds do not do the work of men, and that lilies do not do the work of women? This makes sense only if it is applied to men and women who have left their ordinary work for the sake of the kingdom of God. The text probably originally referred to itinerant radicals. This interpretation was rejected early by the monastic tradition, because work was essential for the monks. Later it was rejected by Reformation exegetes, because they considered one's profession to be a calling from God. And it was rejected by modern bourgeois interpretation, because it is simply improper for one not to work. The history of influence shows how working became an essential part of Christian life, so that our predecessors could not see in the texts what they did not want to see. Indirectly it tells us who we are.

Consider also the history of influence of Matt. 14:1-12, the death of John the Baptist and the dance of the unnamed daughter of Herodias. It reflects the changing role of women and also the changing evaluation of dance. While the classical and medieval

8. *De opere Monachorum*, CSEL 41.531–96.
9. Jerome, *Comm. on Matt.* on 6:25 in Corpus Christianorum SL 77.40.
10. Luz, *Matthew 1–7*, 411, nn. 78–81.

interpreters were interested primarily in the role of the *man* Herod as an incorporation of human evil, since the time of Renaissance the daughter, Salome, became more and more the central figure. The dramatic plays of the death of John the Baptist by Hans Sachs or Oscar Wilde, for example, are only late and perfect examples of a whole genre. They show how Salome became more and more the center of the story. Similarly we see in the altar paintings of the late Middle Ages how the dance of Salome was only one element among others, whereas in the Renaissance portraits of Bernardo Luini and Tiziano, for example, Salome became the center, as a beautiful and fascinating woman with only a superficial biblical touch. The women began to emancipate themselves from their neglected existence in the biblical tradition and its history of influence. We observe a similar development in the evaluation of her dance from the stern condemnation of John Chrysostom ("Where dance is, there is the devil")[11] to the eighteenth century, where we find the first explicit protest against ecclesiastical condemnation of sexuality and dance and a corresponding approval of Salome's dancing. Here history of influence is a mirror of cultural history, an example of modern emancipation from the biblical tradition, symbolically represented by an anonymous girl of the Bible who became a central figure in modern secular literature and art. Again, the history of influence of biblical texts tells us a lot about where we are and what we have become. In this case it also poses critical questions to the Christian tradition.

When we want to understand biblical texts, therefore, it is important that we become aware of our own personal, cultural, and political situations and introduce them consciously into the process of understanding, because all this is already present in it and influences it, whether we are aware of such influences or not. Texts, traditions, and values have significance in a concrete situation and for concrete people or they have no significance at all. The investigation of the history of influence of the texts can make a decisive contribution to the understanding of texts, even though it is a limited contribution and must be supplemented by other approaches, for example, sociological and psychological reflections.

11. *Hom. on Matt.* 48.3.

Ecumenical Dimensions

The study of the history of influence gives access to a great treasure of experiences of other churches and other Christians. Particularly important are interpretations that present corrective models to customary interpretations and applications of one's own tradition and church. At this point, the history of influence has an important ecumenical function: it opens the eyes for new potentials of the texts. It shows not only what we have become through the texts but also what we could have been and what we could become.

For the interpretation of the Sermon on the Mount, and partly also for the missionary discourse of Matthew 10, paradigms from the monastic and from the early Anabaptist traditions were important for me. In those traditions the practice of the gospel was understood in a very Matthean way as an integral part of the gospel itself. Proclaiming the gospel means doing good deeds, so that the people praise God on account of the *works* of the Christians (Matt. 5:16). In the protocols of the disputations of the Reformers with the Anabaptists we discover how well the latter—simple, theologically uneducated farmers and laypeople—understood the basic elements of Matthean theology: the priority of practice before teaching, the will to obedience, the fact that Jesus' commands are taken literally and seriously. On the other hand, it is astonishing how much the distinction between gospel and law as fundamental theological categories made a true perception of Matthean theology impossible in the Reformation, particularly in the Lutheran theological tradition. From the second generation of the Reformation, the gospel was interpreted more or less along Pauline lines.[12] The Anabaptist interpretation, however, is faithful to Matthew's ethical radicalism by interpreting the will of the heavenly Father literally. This message could be a real challenge in our present situation. The commandments of Jesus or God as the center of the Christian message might be essential in a situation in which we are totally dominated by other laws—for instance, the law of productivity, profit, and free enterprise on the basis of the struggle of everybody

---

12. A recent and in his way excellent example: H. Weder, *Die Rede der Reden* (Zürich: Theologischer Verlag Zürich, 1985).

against everybody. The proclamation to return unconditionally to the laws of Jesus might be a fundamental theology of liberation for Western people today. The nucleus of Matthew's theology is that God's law is the gospel! It is a theology that was constantly obscured and pushed aside in the churches of the Reformation, but it may need to be heard by us.

Greek Orthodox traditions were important for my reading of the story of the transfiguration (Matt. 17:1-13).[13] Only there did I find the basic idea of the *participation* of the disciples (and readers) in the vision of Jesus' glory on the mountain. Only there was the mystical experience of the listeners and readers taken seriously as the basis of understanding. In the Orthodox tradition, the transfiguration, the metamorphosis, is one of the great annual festivals of the church. In the cult, the participants go mystically with Jesus onto the mountain and come back again to the world of suffering and acting. This interpretation too, which is linked with an experience in worship, could be a real challenge for people living in a tradition of interpretation dominated by the Enlightenment, where the question of what "really" happened on the mount of transfiguration became dominant. This led to looking at the biblical story as a report about a strange event that urgently needs explanation. With this question, interpreters are unable to grasp the reality toward which our story wants to guide its readers.

The Fruits the Texts Produce Throughout History

For Matthew a word reveals its truth when it brings fruit in the life of the listeners. Those who say "Lord, Lord" but bring forth no corresponding fruits (Matt. 7:21-23) are rejected. The study of the history of effects looks for the fruit of the texts in the course of history, thus posing a very Matthean question. Those who consider these fruits as a possible criterion of truth for a text of a new interpretation are thinking along Matthean lines.[14]

13. See Luz, *Matthäus II*, 514–17.
14. See below, chap. 5.

Naturally those fruits that are ambivalent or negative are particularly interesting. One of the most striking examples is Matt. 27:25, "His blood be on us and on our children." This text has produced untold suffering, even when Christians condemned Israel only theologically and did not proceed to do discriminatory and murderous acts on the assumption of a divine condemnation of Israel. Ancient anti-Semitism and Christian anti-Judaism melted together and created this climate of European anti-Semitism, which finally led to the catastrophe of the Holocaust. I am sorry to say that Matthean theology is one of the many elements that made this disaster possible.

Let me give another example, Matt. 12:31-32, the famous passage about the sin against the Holy Spirit. Go to the psychiatric clinics and look at the hospital reports of mentally ill religious people, or read biographies of devoted Christians who were tortured by doubts about whether or not they had committed this terrible, unforgivable sin of Christians![15] Then you may see what kind of negative fruit biblical texts can bring forward. Does the history of influence unmask a basic deficit of these texts themselves? Or is it possible to separate the texts from what they have caused? Only a very careful historical, sociological, psychological, and theological analysis can attempt to answer such a question. The history of effects shows that texts have power and therefore cannot be separated from their consequences. Interpreting a text is not simply playing with words but an act with historical consequences.

The last example is central. The radical command to love one's enemies in the last antithesis of the Sermon on the Mount (Matt. 5:43-48) is—not only according to Tertullian—the "principal commandment"[16] of Christianity. The history of Christianity is, as we all know, far from a history of love of enemies; examples to the contrary are numerous. Even Matthew himself seems to have completely forgotten what he had written in the Sermon on the Mount when he was writing his twenty-third chapter, with the harsh and unjust woes against Pharisees and scribes. What does that mean?

15. See Luz, *Matthäus II*, 264, n. 88.
16. *De Patientia* 6.

Does it show only how far sinful Christians could be from the truth of the gospel? Or is it a critical question regarding the truth or wisdom of this command? C. G. Montefiore once said that if Christian ethics would not have been so absolute and perfectionist, its results would have been more solid[17] and more supportable for the Jews. Sigmund Freud presumed that the absolute commandment of love caused feelings of guilt and corresponding feelings of aggression toward the outside world.[18] Again, much psychological and sociological investigation would be necessary to approach an answer. I must leave the question as it is. It is important to see that the history of effects excludes the possibility of separating texts or their interpretations from their historical consequences. It prevents mere literalism in interpretation and helps avert the separation of merely theological truths from concrete and historical truths. The study of the history of effects, therefore, leads to questions concerning the truth of biblical texts. But it does not answer them.

A Reevaluation of the Classical Hermeneutics of the Church

We turn now to the history of exegesis of the texts in its proper and narrow sense. My occupation with the history of interpretation has led me to a new evaluation of the hermeneutics of the ancient church and of the Reformation. I mentioned earlier that as I examined and commented on the Matthean texts, the classical commentaries like those of Origen, Hilary, and Jerome, medieval scholars like Albertus Magnus and Thomas Aquinas, and the commentaries of the sixteenth and the seventeenth centuries like those of John Calvin, Johann Brenz, Cornelius a Lapide, and Abraham Calov gave me much more insight into the significance of the texts than most of the modern historical-critical commentaries of today. The late philosopher Georg Picht had the same impression. He said, "Not only the fathers of the church, but already the New Testament Scriptures themselves have risked instances of exegesis

17. C. G. Montefiore, *The Synoptic Gospels II* (London: Macmillan, 1927) 86.
18. S. Freud, *Civilisation and Its Discontents* (London: Hogarth Press, 1951) 81–93.

that must make the hair of every philologian stand on end. But who would dare to doubt that they knew better than we their real subject matter?"[19] Why is that so? It is my impression that the hermeneutics of the fathers is, in many respects, closer to the New Testament texts than that of modern historical-critical interpretation.

It might be helpful to allude briefly to classic patristic hermeneutics. Its father, Origen, Platonist as he was, differentiated between the letter of Scripture, which corresponded to its historical sense or to its "flesh," and the spirit of Scripture. For him, the letter—the historical sense—was a "shadow" or "symbol" of the true, spiritual meaning of Scripture, the eternal gospel. Allegorical interpretation was the tool Christians with perfect knowledge used to understand this spiritual meaning. This spiritual meaning of Scripture is not just a simple consequence of Origen's Platonist worldview or of his gnostic devaluation of the visible world.[20] Rather it corresponds to Christ himself, the eternal, invisible Logos who became flesh. For Origen, interpreting a text meant to help ensure "that the Logos takes shape in the church and in every Christian."[21] Allegorical interpretation helped open the eyes of the readers to the presence of the eternal Logos, Jesus Christ, in the world. Therefore it is clear that the literal, historical interpretation of Scripture is not simply replaceable by allegorical interpretation. Historical interpretation remains true, though less important than the spiritual interpretation, in the same way as the eternal Logos finally prevails over the human appearance of Jesus. Thus Origen's concept of the double meaning of Scripture corresponds to his Christology, namely, the nascent Christology of the two natures. It is, according to 2 Cor. 3:17, the Lord, who is the Spirit, that guides the interpretation.[22]

This christological basis of the interpretation of Scripture was accentuated differently in later times but remained a common basis

19. G. Picht, "Theologie in der Krise der Wissenschaft," *Evangelische Kommentare* (Stuttgart: Kreuz Verlag, 1970) 3.202.
20. I follow the interpretations of H. De Lubac, *Geist aus der Geschichte: Das Schriftverständnis des Origenes* (Einsiedeln: Johannes, 1968) 87–97; and J. Pietron, *Geistige Schriftauslegung und biblische Predigt* (Düsseldorf: Patmos, 1969) 33–120.
21. Pietron, *Geistige Schriftauslegung,* 118.
22. See ibid., 124.

of patristic exegesis. Among the Greek fathers, particularly in the exegesis of Athanasius and Cyril of Alexandria, the incarnation and the union of the two natures became the central clue to the interpretation of Scripture. The possibility of two basic meanings of Scripture, the historical and the pneumatic, "transfers the mystery of Christ to biblical hermeneutics." Johannes Panagopulos, who is currently working on a history of Greek Orthodox biblical interpretation and to whom I owe this quotation, also formulates the consequences of this hermeneutical basis for the interpretation of Scripture: "The concentration of the exegesis of the church upon the person of Jesus Christ . . . has as a consequence that the interpretation is not limited to the language and the text of the Bible alone. . . . Finally the exegetes of the church are concerned about the presence of Christ, his activity in the history of the universe, and about a living encounter with his whole person."[23] It is finally not the biblical texts but the reality of Christ that permeates and shapes the texts that is the ultimate subject matter of all interpretative efforts. Therefore neither the interpreters' exegesis and faith nor their intellectual recognition of a text and their acknowledgment of its relevance can be separated, because the living Christ, the reality in and behind the text, is also living and acting in the process of interpretation. The analogy between Christ and Scripture is an important element also in the classical hermeneutics of the Reformation. There, Scripture and the incarnation of Christ correspond to one another.

This christological and pneumatic exegesis is fascinating and far from being merely allegorical amusement. It means:

1. When all the biblical texts are expressions of a present reality, the living Christ, then every interpretation is guided by our experience and understanding of this living Christ. There is an element of personal identity and personal faith that belongs to all interpretations of biblical texts. They are not "alien" to the interpreter.

2. When the biblical texts become expressions of the living Christ, the barrier between past and present that we experience is

---

23. J. Panagopulos, "Christologie und Schriftauslegung bei den griechischen Kirchenvätern," *ZTK* 89 (1992) 54.

eliminated. Christ, about whom the texts speak, never is a merely past reality. There is no possibility of a "mere" past that has nothing to do with us.

3. When the biblical texts become expressions of the living Christ, they speak with one voice, the voice of the living Christ of faith. Therefore they do not fall apart into many different, unconnected, or even contradicting testimonies of different biblical witnesses, between which modern interpreters have to choose. There is no possibility of dissolving the unity of the biblical message into various different, unconnected testimonies of different people in different situations, which makes the question of the integrity of the Bible so difficult for us.

In sum, the three main problems of historical criticism, which are so burdensome for us and which make the use of the historically reconstructed texts so difficult, do not occur in this hermeneutical model. These three great difficulties are: the barrier between past and present, the barrier between objective meaning of a text and personal interpretation, and the problem of plurality in the Bible itself.

We shall see later that this christological interpretation of Scripture comes very close to the reinterpretation of the Jesus-traditions in the Gospels. For Matthew and the other evangelists, the present Christ was the living force and central principle that reshaped the traditional words of the Jesus-traditions and filled them with new significance and new life. The New Testament reinterpretation of traditions means that the living Christ speaks again through his old words and stories. But this christological interpretation of the New Testament and the early church is very different from our historical-critical exegesis. It would be naive to dismiss the many christological allegories of ecclesiastical exegesis as "exegetically wrong" without realizing the basic truth behind them. This hermeneutic is a challenge for us, but I know quite well that we cannot imitate it and that we cannot, after the Enlightenment and Historicism, simply get rid of our own historical consciousness. The Enlightenment has brought us to a new understanding of autonomy and freedom of the human subject, and historical criticism also is an expression of it. I think we have to try something analogous to this classical christological hermeneutic.

Our principal hermeneutical problem will be to relate our modern understanding of history as a unique and unrepeatable past with the living Jesus Christ, who is the same throughout history and who would live anew through our interpretations and applications of the biblical texts.

THREE

ITINERANT RADICALS, SETTLED COMMUNITIES, AND THE CHURCH TODAY (MATTHEW 10)

In order to make some aspects of my ideas about the history of effects more concrete, let us consider the so-called mission discourse of Matthew 10. This sermon is fundamental for Matthew, because here for the first time the ecclesiological perspective of the Gospel becomes clear. However, its history of effects was not of fundamental importance for the church, neither in the past, nor in the present. The history of interpretation is meager, and also today there is very little interest inside and outside the churches in this passage. What does that reveal about our own situation? And, conversely, what kind of challenge and corrective could this text have for our churches today?

The Fundamental Importance of the Mission Discourse

One of the basic assumptions of the history of this text's interpretation was that this sermon was concerned only about Jesus' first commissioning of his disciples during his ministry. The first to put forward this interpretation was Tertullian,[1] and it has remained popular up to this day.[2] If this interpretation is correct, this sermon

1. *Fuga* 6.1 in Corpus Christianorum SL 2.1142.
2. For instance, G. Strecker, *Der Weg der Gerechtigkeit* (FRLANT 82; Göttingen: Vandenhoeck & Ruprecht, 1962) 196; A. Vögtle, "Das christologische und ekklesiologische Anliegen von Mt 28:16-20," in idem, *Das Evangelien und die Evangelien* (KBANT; Düsseldorf: Patmos, 1971) 166.

speaks not about the church but only about a unique event in the past of Jesus. With this assumption, many problems could be solved. Almost never in its history has the church resembled what is here described, and almost never has the church followed what is here prescribed. The church has not consisted of itinerant radicals; quite the contrary, the radicals, whenever they existed, were considered suspect. This was especially true in the times of the orders of mendicant friars in the late Middle Ages, and again in the Reformation, when the Anabaptists were considered to be a danger for the churches. Calvin, more than others, stressed that Matthew 10 was not setting up timeless laws but was exclusively intended for the first mission of the disciples. He said: Because they had only a few days for their mission to Israel, Jesus told them to leave their luggage at home and to travel light.[3]

In modern exegesis, three arguments were important in supporting the assumption that Matthew 10 was intended for the time of Jesus only:

1. Jesus sends out the twelve *apostles*. These twelve apostles are unique figures of the past.

2. The prohibition to go to the Gentiles and to the Samaritans (vv. 5-6) and the announcement that the disciples will not finish their flight through the cities of Israel (v. 23) do not correspond with the reality of Matthew's church, which is sent to missionize the Gentiles.

3. Verses 17-22 are interesting, because Matthew has used here a part of the Synoptic apocalypse, namely, Mark 13:9-13, and has moved it forward. In chapter 24 this section is repeated in a slightly more general form. Does this mean that Matthew speaks about two persecutions of the disciples, one during the lifetime of Jesus in the past (chap. 10) and one in his own time among the Gentiles (chap. 24)?

Such an interpretation of Matthew 10 is not only very popular but also very convenient. It would help us to solve many problems. But I don't think it is correct, and I am inclined to think that such interpretations—in the past and maybe also in the present—are,

3. J. Calvin, *Auslegung der Evangelienharmonie I* (ed. H. Stadtland-Neumann and H. Vogelbusch; Neukirchen-Vluyn: Neukirchener Verlag, 1966) 291, 295f.

consciously or unconsciously, wishful thinking. Let me here mention some arguments against it.

1. All the other discourses of the Matthean Gospel are "spoken out of the window." That means that they are not part of the narrative only, but they transcend the narrative and address the hearers or readers of the Gospel directly. Why should this sermon be the only exception?

2. The addressees of the sermon are not only the twelve apostles but, at the same time, the disciples (10:1; 11:1). *Disciple* seems to function as a transparent term in the Gospel. The readers identify with the disciples, and, in that way, they take part in the history of Jesus and hear his words. There seems to be no difference between the "historical" term *apostle* and the "transparent" term *disciple*. And this is good Matthean theology because, for Matthew, to be a disciple means contemporaneity: to become contemporary with Jesus at every time, to learn from him, to follow him, and to be protected by him. The church of all times has to follow the way of the earthly Jesus; it cannot separate itself from this unique master and Lord of the past.[4]

3. None of the logia of our chapter, with the exceptions of verses 5f. and 23, exhibits any trace that it was meant only for a limited time in the past. Rather all seem to have a timeless relevance for the church of all times, which cannot expect a better fate than that of its master (cf. vv. 24f.). This is particularly true of verses 17-22, the passage transferred from the Markan apocalypse to our chapter.

4. The mission discourse is a discourse and not part of a report, as in Mark 6:7-13, 30 and possibly also in Q (cf. Luke 10:17-20). In Matthew the disciples never leave Jesus and never go away on the mission. At the end of the discourse, Matthew says that *Jesus* went away from there to teach and preach in their towns (11:1). If it would be limited to the past, Matthew would have taken over the Markan report of the commissioning of the disciples.

5. The relationship of the discourse with other parts of the Gospel, particularly the Sermon on the Mount, is very close. The

---

4. See U. Luz, "The Disciples in the Gospel according to Matthew," in *The Interpretation of Matthew* (ed. G. Stanton; Issues in Religion and Theology 3; Philadelphia: Fortress Press; London: SPCK, 1983) 98–114.

disciples preach the same message as Jesus preached (v. 7; cf. 4:17). Their behavior corresponds to the commandments in the Sermon on the Mount (cf. 5:38-42 and 10:10, 16; 5:10-12 and 10:16f.; 6:25-34 and 10:28-30, etc.). The Sermon on the Mount definitely is not meant only for the past time of Jesus; it is the "gospel of the kingdom" to be preached to the Gentiles.

My thesis is therefore that Matthew 10 as a whole is of fundamental importance for Matthew. In this chapter Matthew extends and actualizes the mission of Jesus in Israel (chaps. 8–9) and extends also the fundamental proclamation of Jesus into the life of his disciples, thus describing the life of the future church. Matthew 10 is the ecclesiological prolongation of chapters 5–9. This observation was seldom made in the history of interpretation.

There remains the problem of verses 5f. and 23. I think they have the special function of rooting the discourse in Matthew's narrative. Matthew describes how Jesus was the healing and loving Messiah of his people Israel, how the leaders of Israel and finally the whole people rejected this Messiah, so that he had to withdraw with his disciples from Israel. Apart from Israel the disciples became a special group that accompanied Jesus and was instructed by him. Matthew then, in chapters 21–28, narrates Jesus' great settling of accounts with Israel and how Israel finally rejected Jesus in the passion, so that the risen Lord sent his disciples to the Gentiles. At the time of chapter 10 Jesus was still working in Israel, and the church apart from Israel did not yet exist. Verses 5f. and 23 are a reminder of this.

Basic "Notes"[5] of the Church according to Matthew

I would like to try now a systematic interpretation of our text and to allude, by contrast, to some references on the history of interpretation. They can show us what we have rejected or forgotten and, through that, what we have become today. They also help to point out the situation where we must face the text.

---

5. The expression is borrowed from the Reformation *notae ecclesiae*. See the section in this chapter on "The Matthean 'Notes' and Our Ecclesiologies," 50ff.

1. In Matthew 10 the church appears as a missionizing, proclaiming church. However, it is striking to observe how little our chapter tells us about the *content* of the disciples' proclamation. The short note in verse 7 takes up 4:17 and shows that the disciples have to carry on the proclamation of Jesus. Besides that, the entire sermon is a discourse about the behavior and the destiny of the disciples, about their life-style and their suffering. This is the most astonishing feature of the whole chapter and demands a theological explanation. Theological ideas about the essence of the church were evidently not important for Matthew; the life of the church was what mattered to him.

A particularly striking feature of our chapter is the emphasis Jesus gives to healing as an integral part of the disciples' mission (v. 8). Preaching and healing are of equal importance for Matthew. The history of interpretation exhibits a general tendency to relativize or downplay the miracles and the healings in the church. To limit them to the beginnings of Christianity, to the time of Jesus or the apostles, was only one possible way to get rid of them. Jerome thought that the apostles were simple people who lacked good theological and homiletical training; therefore they received the gift of healing as compensation.[6] Frequently the healings were spiritualized: to become free of the bondage of sin is the greatest healing miracle.[7] But the most common way to interpret verse 8 was to pass over it in silence. At this point, the history of interpretation in all the main churches is an exact mirror of what the churches were and are.

2. A second characteristic of which I found not one echo in the history of interpretation: the church appears in our chapter as a group of *itinerant radicals*, at least in the first part (vv. 1-23). Jesus sends his disciples off traveling. If the transparency of the disciples in the Matthean Gospel is taken seriously, the church of Matthew should be a group of itinerant radicals. But the discourse has odd fluctuations. Up to verse 23 we find several references to the disciples' traveling. From verse 24 on, these notions disappear; verses 24-39 can be applied equally to itinerants and to Christians in settled

6. *Comm. on Matt.* in Corpus Christianorum SL 77.65.
7. J. Chrysostom, *Hom. on Matt.* 32.8.

communities. The final section, verses 40-42, begins with a promise to the travelers (v. 40), but then the perspective changes: in verses 41f., those at home are addressed. How is this fluctuation to be understood?

Palestinian Christianity originated as a movement of itinerant radicalism. Its roots go back to Jesus; the disciples he called to follow him and to witness to the imminent kingdom of God as he did shared his style of life and were poor and homeless. They gave up their jobs and their family for the time they were together with Jesus. After their master's death many of them continued this way of life.

Unlike Gerd Theissen, to whom we owe most of our knowledge of these forgotten origins of early Christianity, I think that it is not possible to make a clear distinction between the itinerant radicals and the adherents of Jesus in settled communities. The distinction was rather fluid in the whole of early Christianity, as itinerant radicals founded congregations and maintained the contacts between them. They settled in these congregations, and others were sent out for the missionary work, as reflected, for instance, in Acts 13:1-3, in 3 John, and in *Didache* 11–13. The old principle in Q that a worker deserves his wages (Matt. 10:9; Luke 10:7; cf. 1 Cor. 9:4) shows that the radicals were recognized by the settled congregations as *their* workers; the congregations identified themselves with their missionaries and took responsibility for them.[8]

I think that the Matthean church lived in close contact with itinerant radicals and participated both in their mission and in the hospitality to the missionaries. For Matthew, both itinerant radicals and resident Christians were "disciples" who "followed" Jesus. Perhaps we can say that, for Matthew, all members of his congregations were potential itinerant radicals.[9] He sees the Christians as being on the way to perfection, moving toward a higher righteousness (5:20, 48). On this way, itinerant radicalism with absolute poverty might have been thought of as one example of "higher"

---

8. See U. Luz, "Die Kirche und ihr Geld im Neuen Testament," in *Die Finanzen der Kirche* (ed. W. Lienemann; Munich: Kaiser, 1989) 537f.
9. See U. Luz, *Das Evangelium nach Matthäus II (Mt 8–17)* (EKKNT I/2; Neukirchen-Vluyn: Neukirchener; Zürich: Benziger, 1990) 78f.

righteousness. But texts like Matt. 19:23ff. show that all the disciples—not only an elite—are called to this form of existence. Matthew does not distinguish between two classes of Christians, as, for example, the later Syrian Liber Graduum did. His idea is that of Christian life as a course in which everyone should move ahead, as far as she or he is able. In a similar way the *Didache* says: "If you cannot carry the whole yoke of the Lord, do what you can" (*Did* 6:2). Therefore, on one hand, itinerancy for the sake of mission is an essential mark of a Christian. On the other hand, it is not a precondition of being a disciple, because it is only the judge of the world who will decide finally whose righteousness was "greater than that of the Pharisees and scribes" (5:20).

And what about the history of effects of this concept? It is brief. Apart from some monastic traditions, particularly in Syria, where itinerant radicalism became a characteristic of Christian asceticism and virginity, the idea of itinerant radicalism disappeared almost entirely. Only for the mendicant monks and preachers in the Middle Ages did it become the model of their *via apostolica*. Today we owe our awareness of early Christian itinerant radicalism almost entirely to Gerd Theissen. This means that, until now, the churches were extremely successful in ignoring it. No wonder: A church that constructs cathedrals and that offers not only food but both houses and cars to its workers cannot appreciate this kind of tradition.

3. A third point is the poverty of the disciples. In our discourse, Matthew refers to it in verses 8b-10. Here he emphasizes especially in the traditional rule of equipment of missionaries that they should not "earn" gold, that is, they should not be paid for their mission, healings, and exorcisms. At the same time, he takes over from the tradition the old rule of absolute poverty and defenselessness: no bag, no second tunic, no staff. For Matthew, it is impossible not only to earn money through preaching the kingdom of heaven but also to do this in good shoes, with a bag full of provisions, and with a staff against wild animals or bandits. Looking through the whole Gospel, I have the impression that the idea not only of defenselessness but also of poverty is more important for Matthew than is generally thought. The section immediately after the center of the Sermon on the Mount (6:19-34), which has to be interpreted

as *one* coherent section about problems of mammon and poverty, is devoted to this matter. Also important are the explanation of the seed among the thorns (13:22) and the parables of the treasure and the pearl (13:44-46). In verses 44-46 Matthew's preoccupation is not that finding is the first act[10] but that selling all the possessions is the second. The problem of possessions and poverty is the only concrete admonition we find in the chapter of parables. Consider also 16:24-26, where self-denial clearly means to renounce the gaining of the whole world, and 19:16-30, where to renounce one's possessions belongs to the command to follow Jesus and is interpreted as an act of loving one's neighbor and as a characteristic of Christian perfection. Matthew 19:24-29 makes it clear that every disciple is called to become poor.

What about the history of effects? Matthew 10:8-10 *had* effects in history: it became the decisive text in the life of Francis of Assisi[11] and a decisive characteristic for the *via apostolica* of Peter Waldo and his followers.[12] But the history of interpretation of this text in the mainline churches is a history of bypassing or annulment by means of reinterpretation. The text was taken literally almost exclusively as a polemical weapon against ecclesiastical opponents living in luxury.[13] It was often softened by interpreting it as a nonprovision rule—the itinerants do not need any provisions, because they can rely on the hospitality of friendly houses like the Essenes.[14] It has been very popular to mention Paul, whose mission had a different character; Heinrich Bullinger, for example, knew that at least Paul did possess shoes,[15] or Jerome learned from Platon that the apostles used sandals, which are much more convenient than heavy boots.[16] It was also popular to moralize the text, so that the intention is

10. J. D. Crossan, *Finding Is the First Act* (Semeia Supplement; Philadelphia: Fortress Press, 1979).

11. See W. Goez, "Franciscus von Assisi," (*TRE* 11; Missoula: Scholars Press, 1983) 300; "Regula non Bullata," 8.14 ("The Earlier Rule," in *Francis and Clare, The Complete Works*, trans. R. Armstrong and I. C. Brady [New York: Paulist Press, 1982]) 116, 120.

12. K.-V. Selge, *Die ersten Waldenser I* (AKG 37.1; Berlin: Walter de Gruyter 1967) 49f., 116f.

13. Luz, *Matthäus II*, 98, n. 64.

14. See Josephus, *J.W.* 2.124–26.

15. *In Sacrosanctum . . . Evangelium secundum Matthaeum Comm libri XII* (Zürich: Froschauer, 1546) 99.

16. *Comm. on Matt.* in Corpus Christiamorum SL 77, 66.

said to be the prevention of pride or avarice. Ulrich Zwingli interprets it as a call for a middle way between the luxury of the pope and the total rejection of salaries of preachers in early Anabaptism.[17] In the disputations between Reformed preachers and Anabaptist lay preachers in the sixteenth century, Luke 10:7 was an argument that ministers must have a regular salary![18] Allegorical interpretation was used to bypass the existential and ecclesiastical difficulties of a literal interpretation: going barefoot meant not to cover the gospel; having only one tunic (*chitōn*) meant knowing Christ and nobody else.[19] Let me mention a final example of more recent times: churches in many European countries, particularly in West Germany and Switzerland, are rather wealthy, because their financing system is based on taxes. Salaries of most ministers in Germany and Switzerland are high. In Germany we have too many students of theology; several hundred young theologians are unemployed and cannot find a job in the church. However, I was unable to find a single reminiscence of our text in the discussions of the churches. The possibility of lowering a minister's salary to employ more people seems to be taboo. It looks as if Matt. 10:8-10 and parallels has gone among the secret Gospels!

4. The fourth point concerns suffering as a characteristic of discipleship. Here we are in the center of our discourse. In verses 17-23, 28f. and verses 34-39 Matthew speaks about the perspectives of suffering. Suffering is important for him. The center of his discourse is the christological statement in verses 24-25: No servant is greater than his or her master. The life of the disciples has to be the same as the life of Jesus. Therefore Matthew uses "Jesus language" in his words about suffering. In verses 17-21 he uses "to hand over" as a "key word"; the disciples will be "handed over" to their persecutors, as Christ was handed over in his passion. In verse 38 he speaks about the "cross" of the disciples, again reminding us of Jesus and his cross. Even if the "cross" in verse 38 no longer directly refers to the death of the disciples but has become a metaphor for suffering, in verse 39 the martyrdom of the disciples

17. *Annotationes in Evangelium Matthaei* (Opera VI/1; ed. M. Schuler and J. Schulthess; Zürich: Schulthess, 1836) 265.
18. Luz, *Matthäus II*, 100, n. 85.
19. Ibid., 98, n. 65.

is the perspective of their life. "To lose one's life" cannot be interpreted differently. The christological allusions make clear that the disciples must suffer, and this not just accidentally in an unfortunate situation. Suffering, for Matthew, is a real hallmark of discipleship.

What about the history of influence? Let me take verses 38-39 as an example. There are some interpreters who took the radical character of verses 38-39 seriously, but not many. More typical was a generalizing interpretation, which took its point of departure from the Markan form of the word and his idea of self-denial. Self-denial could be interpreted in a general way in the sense of every suffering and pain but also in the sense of ascetic practices on the way to perfection. In this case therefore we cannot say that our word was rejected in the history of interpretation, but rather that it was widened or reinterpreted in an individualistic and ascetic context.

5. This last characteristic of discipleship leads us to the core of Matthew's ecclesiology: *Discipleship means life in Christ's pattern.* For Matthew, the story of Jesus is the key to the missionary discourse. To live and to suffer as Jesus did is for Matthew the most important "note" of the church. This is why a discourse that seeks to deal with the mission of the disciples speaks almost exclusively about their life, their obedience, and their suffering. Jesus' authority and the power to heal is handed over to the disciples. Jesus' own preaching and teaching are the content of their message. Their life of poverty corresponds to the life of the Son of man, of whom Matthew said shortly before that he had no place to lay his head (8:19). Being unarmed, being itinerant—these were marks of Jesus' existence. The suffering of the disciples is a reenactment of the suffering and death of Jesus. In one sentence, the lot of disciples should reflect that of the master; and a servant cannot expect anything better than his or her Lord (10:24f.)

This corresponds to Matthean Christology: Matthew tells the story of Jesus as a basic model of life. He is the obedient Son of God who fulfills all justice (3:15) and the Law and the Prophets (5:17). This obedient Son of God endured hostility and persecution, and finally he suffered and died (27:43, 54). The Matthean missionary discourse transfers the model of Jesus to the disciples.

It corresponds to the Matthean understanding of proclamation as well. The disciples are the light of the world, which shines in their works and for the sake of which people praise the heavenly Father (5:14-16). Not only what the disciples say but what they do and what they suffer—what they *are*—has proclamatory character. And it corresponds to the Matthean understanding of judgment: for Matthew, the final judgment depends entirely on the fruits (7:15-20). The mere words of those who know that Jesus is the Lord do not count; only enacting the law of love does (7:21-23).

In most cases the history of interpretation made our texts easier, generalized them, or even pushed them aside. This background shows that these texts were relevant for the churches. But because the reality of the churches did not correspond to the reality of the texts, very often the interpretations served as an excuse or an alibi. The history of influence reminds us of the deficits of our churches vis-à-vis the New Testament, and this leads us to an understanding of our own ecclesiastical situation.

6. Can the history of effects also offer us correctives and alternative models? Does it help toward a directional meaning of our text for today? In this case, it is the text itself that offers corrective models; the history of interpretation plays a secondary role. The main difficulty is that the respective situations have changed so much. Many of us feel sympathy for the early Christian itinerants and would concede to their form of living a high degree of authenticity. Probably all of us feel sympathies for Francis of Assisi, for Peter Waldo and his followers, or for the early Anabaptists. But it is immediately clear that we cannot copy their model simply and directly. If we would become radically poor and itinerant, we would be authentic, but probably not much more than that. Our testimony for the kingdom of God today requires a somewhat different form of embodiment and testimony through life.

The study of the history of influence therefore also makes clear to us the difference between the situation of the text and our own situation and prevents a premature leap over the chasm of the centuries. This text requires a new interpretation today. When we think our text and its history of influence does not offer us directly corrective models, then we have to ask what kind of directional meaning the Matthean sermon has for our understanding and the life of the church in our situation. To question the *direction* that a text points is something more fundamental than to state this or that application. Our text does not give us simple prescriptions but a basic direction for a new ecclesiology. Therefore I would like to reflect now about the question of the kind of ecclesiologies that prevented Matthew 10 from becoming a fundamental text in the course of the history of the church even though it is a fundamental ecclesiological text of the New Testament. Only then can we realize the depth of our text's ecclesiological challenge.

The Matthean "Notes" and Our Ecclesiologies

When I speak about the Matthean "notes" of the church, I am borrowing a term from the dogmatic tradition of the Reformation. "Notes" are the fundamental characteristics that identify the visible church in the ambiguity of this world. I use this word because I now want to contrast the Matthean concept of the church and our own ecclesiological tradition on a fundamental level. Our tradition has neglected many of the challenges of the Matthean text. Why? One of the basic reasons is that our own dominant concepts of what the church is prevented us from recognizing the fundamental character of Matthew's ecclesiology. It is not the model of the church as a community of disciples that stamped our Protestant or Roman Catholic churches but another model of thought—namely, the Augustinian distinction between the visible and the invisible church. Both Roman Catholic and Protestant ecclesiologies see the visible church in relation to the invisible, cosmic, heavenly, true church. Christologically this means that the risen, exalted Christ is fundamental for the church, and not, as in Matthew, the earthly Jesus, his life and his destiny. This is apparent in the New Testament, where the church is understood as the body of Christ in the Pauline and Deutero-Pauline epistles. This concept transcends the visible, earthly church and emphasizes its cosmic dimensions and its participation in eternal life. The relationship between the visible and the invisible church is differently accentuated in Protestant and Roman Catholic ecclesiologies.

Protestant ecclesiology interprets the visible church according to the Augsburg Confession as "the assembly of saints in which the Gospel is taught purely and the sacraments are administered rightly."[20] The proclaimed gospel and the two sacraments are the only *notae ecclesiae* that are characteristic marks of the visible church in the ambiguity of the world. In a similar way, Calvin takes the pure preaching of the word of God and the sacraments administered according to the institution of Christ as the two *symbola* of the church.[21] That this definition is typical of the Reformation becomes clear when we observe what is *not* characteristic of the true church. Human deeds or human praxis are not decisive notes of the church, because it would be contrary to justification by faith alone, if anything that human beings make out of the church would be constitutive for it. The visible church is constituted only by the gifts of God. Particularly Calvin and Philipp Melanchthon emphasize that the visible church is not characterized by its own holiness or righteousness. The "illusion of a perfect holiness" destroys the church.[22] The examples of the Donatists and the Anabaptists illustrate what the Reformers fought against. On the other hand, neither a certain external constitution nor ceremonies nor a certain hierarchical or synodical structure is constitutive for the church. In this way the Reformers wanted to keep the door open for a dialogue with the Roman Catholic church. According to them, the point is not that the Catholic church is no church because of its ceremonies or structure but simply that the structure of the church and its ceremonies, essential for the Roman Catholic church, are adiaphora for the Reformers.

The difficulty of this concept of *notae ecclesiae* is that the Reformers' definition of the visible church did not lead to a real distinction between true and false churches in the world. It was able only to prevent rashly formed distinctions. Who is to decide which proclamation corresponds to the true gospel? What if, for hundreds

---

20. The Augsburg Confession, Article VII, *The Book of Concord*, trans. and ed. T. G. Tappert (Philadelphia: Fortress Press, 1959) 32 (trans. from Latin text).
21. Calvin, *Institutes* 4.1.8f.
22. Ibid., 13.

of years, the word of God has been obscured in the church? What if mistakes and useless ceremonies have crept into the administration of the sacraments? Are such mistakes peripheral or central? And what does the basic expression of the Augsburg Confession, "assembly of saints," mean? In the tradition of the Reformation, for various reasons, the idea of the visible church as a mixed body, consisting of good and bad people, true and false believers, became important. Matthew 13:36-43, the explanation of the parable of the tares, is a fundamental text for Reformation ecclesiology. That means that the holiness of the church is not visible, but rather is an attribute that can only be believed and hoped for. Is that enough? Is it accidental that Luther in various writings, for instance, in "On the Councils and the Church," included suffering and persecution among the notes of the church?[23] This was the first time in the ecclesiological tradition of the Reformation that a central Matthean idea entered ecclesiology. In the Reformed tradition after Calvin, discipline or obedience increasingly became a third "note" of the church.[24]

This is the basic problem of Reformation ecclesiology: if the visible church is constituted only by the gifts of God, and if the actual shape of the church in which these gifts become visible is not important, then we have a kind of ecclesiological docetism. Then the true visible church can be separated completely from the actual church in the world. What this church actually looks like—for instance, if it is rich or poor, democratic or hierarchical, a lay-people's church or a theologian's church—and what this church does—for instance, if it is politically engaged or not, if it supports apartheid or socialism or not—is irrelevant as long as the word is preached and the sacraments are administered properly. The Reformation understanding of the church has a dangerous tendency toward idealism and is not really able to define the reality of the church. Such a church has no urgent need to change and reform its praxis, because praxis is not so important and every church is a church of sinners.

23. *Luther's Works*, ed. H. T. Lehmann (Philadelphia: Fortress Press, 1966) 41.138–54.
24. See Calvin, "Responsio ad Sadolet: epistolam" (*Opera Selecta*; ed. P. Barth; Munich: Kaiser, 1926) 1.467.

Catholic ecclesiology also departs from the Augustinian distinction of the visible and the invisible church. For Catholics, however, the true church is visible not only in word and sacrament but also in its institutional forms. The supranatural community is at work in the visible office of the bishop, in the visible priesthood, in visible ministry, and in the whole visible body of the church.[25] The Second Vatican Council's constitution on the church identifies the invisible church, which is confessed in the Creed, with the visible Catholic church, which is governed by the successors of Peter and the bishops. Reformation ecclesiology had, as I said, a docetic tendency. This is not the case in Catholic ecclesiology, which follows an incarnational model of thinking. "The church," said Karl Rahner, taking up ideas of *mystici corporis*, "bears marks of the incarnated and of the risen Christ. It is at once visible and invisible, like the Son of God."[26] The visible and the invisible church are united in a mysterious way, analogous to the union of the two natures in Christ.

The difficulty of this concept lies in the fact that the more the visible church is directly identifiable with the invisible church, the more it is in danger of becoming unreformable. The church, interpreted in this way, hypostatizes itself and believes in itself. And again, but in another way, this model of the church makes a static impression—a characteristic feature of every definition of the church that takes its point of departure christologically from the risen Christ or the two natures of Christ.

Matthew's concept of the church is very different. His basic idea is that of the disciples who follow Jesus. In the Protestant or Catholic dogmatic tradition, this is a minor point, usually dealt with in the chapter about sanctification or elsewhere in an ethical chapter. That is one of the reasons why Matthew 10 could not really influence ecclesiology. Naturally there were some communities that understood themselves as disciples following Christ, such as the Franciscans, the Waldensians, the Lollards, and the Anabaptists and

---

25. Draft of Vatican I about the Church of Christ 4 = J. Neuner and H. Roos, *Der Glaube der Kirche* (11th ed.; Regensburg: Pustet, 1989) n. 389.
26. K. Rahner, "Die Gliedschaft in der Kirche nach der Lehre der Enzyklika Pius XII 'Mystici Corporis Christi,' " in idem, *Schriften zur Theologie II* (7th ed.; Einsiedeln: Benziger, 1964) 89.

their successors. If I see it correctly, their characteristic is not that they propagate an ecclesiological model along the lines of discipleship; they usually have no *doctrine* about the church but speak instead about the church's life and practice.

But Matthew wants to do more than simply describe the practice of a church. He confronts us with a fundamentally different, nonidealistic *understanding* of the church. This is the true challenge for us, and from here the directional meaning of Matthew 10 becomes visible. The basis of his concept is not the church's invisible, heavenly nature but rather its power, authority, and task given by its Lord. It is not the church's teaching or sacraments that are its decisive notes, but its life in poverty and defenselessness, its deeds of justice and love, and the consequences for the church, namely, hatred, suffering, and death. Unlike usual Protestant ecclesiology, Matthew achieves something essential: He places the "notes" of the church right into the realm of the concrete world. For Matthew, the church is what it is, not in a realm somewhere beyond the reality of the world, but right in the middle of it, in its justice, love, struggle, and suffering. When Matthew speaks about itinerancy, poverty, defenselessness, and love, he makes concrete the holiness that is given to the church. No tendency toward ecclesiological docetism, no separation of the true church from the real church, no devaluation of the real life of the church is possible for him. Matthew speaks about the real church in the world, as does Catholic ecclesiology. But again, he does it in a completely different way. For him, the church is not something static and primarily institutional. His concept is that of a dynamic church. The church in its institutional appearance is not yet the church, but only in its obedience and its deeds. It is the church insofar as it has a task, authority, and power from its Lord and insofar as it *lives* according to its mission, is obedient, and *practices* what is given and commanded to it. The Matthean concept is that of a dynamic church because Matthew does not know a true, invisible church beyond history but only the real church in history, which is on the way, struggling, working, suffering. Such a church never can absolutize itself, because it—and not only its members—is on the way to the last judgment of the Son of man.

How is the Matthean concept of the church possible? It is possible christologically, because Matthew links the church exclusively with the earthly Jesus. It is possible because Matthew has a narrative theology. He tells the story of Jesus. In this story, the church does not simply exist but *becomes* the church, because Jesus, who heals his people, shares his power with the disciples and gives them a task. The church does not simply exist, but *endures*, because Jesus is with his church in various ways: he strengthens it when its faith becomes weak and instructs it so that it learns what is the will of the Father. The church does not simply exist, but what the church is *will appear*, at the time when the Son of man separates the sheep from the goats within it in order to remind the church one last time that it is not constituted by its own designs. Matthew's narrative does not simply prefigure the activities of the church; it provides a definition of the church. Matthew's story prevents a conceptual definition of the church, because his narrative theology is not simply an ornament or novelistic embellishment of a conceptual theology.

The study of the history of effects, as a bridge between the text and ourselves, can help us to see our own situation more clearly. In the case of Matthew 10, it was primarily the history of noneffects that proved to be important. Matthew 10 had so little effect upon the history of the mainline churches because it could be easily marginalized; it was hardly realized that it is a fundamental ecclesiological text and not simply a description of some peripheral activities of the church. Beyond all the single notes of the church in our text we find something like a basic framework of what the church essentially is: a community *on the way*. It is the church insofar as it *lives* with the gift and the task entrusted to it by Jesus and insofar as it *moves* on Jesus' way of obedience, love, and suffering. This gives a basic direction about how to consider the church today in the light of Matthew. It is not healings, poverty, itinerancy, defenselessness, and sufferings as absolute principles that are constitutive for the church, but rather healings, poverty, itinerancy, defenselessness, and sufferings alone, because such are hallmarks of the way of Jesus that correspond to his history and lead us on our way toward love.

FOUR

PETER: THE TRUE CHRISTIAN OR THE POPE? (MATTHEW 16)

The famous primacy text, Matt. 16:18, has been a storm center of exegesis. Its effects on history are overwhelming. Go to Rome, enter Michelangelo's St. Peter's, lift your eyes, and read this text inscribed in huge letters around the cupola! This is the "petrified" expression of the tremendous effect of our text on subsequent history. Hardly any other text in the New Testament has produced such contradictory effects. The Roman Catholic interpretation, that the rock of the church is Peter and the Roman bishops who succeed him, is only one part of it. In the late Middle Ages and in the time of the Reformation, our text served also as a strong exegetical argument against Roman claims. The interpretations not only vary widely in subsequent history, but some even directly contradict each other. These contradictory interpretations pose the question of truth in interpretation, the principal subject of this chapter and the next.

An Overview of the History of Interpretation

There are four main types of interpretations of Matt. 16:18 in the history of exegesis.

1. The first is the *typological interpretation*, which is not only the oldest that we know of but is also the "mother" of two other

main types of interpretation. We could call it the "democratic" interpretation of Matt. 16:18. Its classical representative is Origen. According to him, Peter symbolizes every true, spiritual Christian. He says, "A rock is every disciple . . . who drank of the spiritual rock [Christ], who followed them" (1 Cor. 10:4).[1] Elsewhere Origen says that the church is built on the word in every human being, and, in this way, every Christian becomes strong like a rock.[2] According to this interpretation, Peter is the type of the true, spiritual, and perfect Christian.

This interpretation was also widespread in Christian Gnosticism. There Peter is the prototype of the true Gnostic, who received his knowledge through revelation from the spiritual world.[3] Even Tertullian, who was decidedly antignostic, also understood the authority given to Peter as the authority of every spiritual Christian.[4]

The typological interpretation was the basis of two other main types of interpretations, the classical Eastern and the classical Western interpretations.

2. *The Eastern interpretation:* In the Greek and Syrian churches, the rock was interpreted as the *confession or the faith of Peter.* Historically this is a development of Origen's typological interpretation. In identifying this rock upon which every perfect spiritual Christian is founded, Origen already pointed to faith.[5] Tertullian also could interpret Peter as the one who guarantees the unaltered and public apostolic tradition.[6] According to Theodore of Mopsuestia, the confession of Peter "does not belong to Peter alone, but was for all people. When Jesus called his confession a rock, he clarified that it is upon this [confession] that he wanted to build his church."[7] This interpretation does not contest that Jesus' promise was given to Peter personally, but it puts the emphasis on the application of this gift. The question was, "How is Peter the rock of the church?"

---

1. *Comm. on Matt.* 12.10 = GCS Origenes 10.86.
2. See *Contra Celsum* 6.77.
3. See *Apocalypse of Peter,* Nag Hammadi Codex VII, 71, 14–72, 4.
4. *De Pudicitia* 21.
5. *Fragment* 345 II = GCS Origenes 12.149.
6. *De Praescriptione Haereticorum* 22.4f.
7. Theodore of Mopsuestia, *Fragment* 92 = J. Reuss, *Matthäuskommentare aus der griechischen Kirche* (TU 61; Berlin: Akademie, 1957) 129.

The answer refers exegetically to his confession in Matt. 16:16. But it is also a contextual answer to the situation of the church in the fourth century. The church then had to defend its true identity by refuting the claims of the heretics. In this situation the basic Christian confession of the divine sonship of Jesus was really the rock upon which the church was built. Also in later centuries, under Islamic dominion, the traditional confession remained the rock of the Eastern churches that secured their identity. This interpretation corresponded not only to the text but also to the needs of the situation.

This interpretation focusing on Peter's confession was widespread not only in the East; Ambrose, Hilary, and Ambrosiaster made it known also in the West. In one of his early writings, Ambrose added the significant observation that Peter had a primacy "of confession . . . , not of honor; . . . of faith, not of order."[8] Here we have a trace of anti-Roman polemics, which was unusual at that time but might have been necessary in northern Italy. The Eastern interpretation remained known and popular in the West throughout the Middle Ages. Usually it had no anti-Roman accent. The reason for this was that the Roman interpretation of our text was so marginal and unknown that it was not necessary to be preoccupied with it. Only in the late Middle Ages, as a protest against pontifical claims, could it be said that the confession of Peter and not Peter himself was the rock.[9] With this new focus, such an interpretation was used also by the Reformers.[10] But it is not, as is often said, *the* Reformation interpretation; it was the most ecumenical interpretation of that time.

What were the functional effects of this interpretation? It strengthened the identity of the church, based on the traditional confession, whereas the earlier Origenistic interpretation strengthened the identity of the individual Christian. That it strengthened the position of the opponents against Rome was only a later side

8. *De Incarnationis dominicae sacramento* 4.32 = CSEL 79.238f.

9. Faber Stapulensis and Erasmus; see U. Luz, *Das Evangelium nach Matthäus II (Mt 8–17)* (EKKNT I/2; Neukirchen-Vluyn: Neukirchener; Zürich: Benziger, 1990) 477 n.160.

10. Zwingli, *Annotations* 321; Melanchthon, *Tractatus de potestate Papae* = Bekenntnisschriften der evangelisch-lutherischen Kirche (4th ed., Göttingen: Vandenhoeck & Ruprecht, 1959) 480.

effect. Their position not to accept the exclusive authority of the pope was justified precisely by referring to Matt. 16:18.

3. Origen and Tertullian are also the ancestors of the other important type of interpretation that dominated the Western exegesis of the Middle Ages, the *christological interpretation*.[11] Its real father is Augustine. For him, the rock of the church is not Peter but Christ himself. Texts like 1 Cor. 10:4 and 1 Cor. 3:11 were decisive for him. Peter is not the rock, but, as a believer in Christ and as the first apostle, he represents the church. It is not, he could say, that the rock took its name from Peter, but Peter had his name from the *petra*, the "rock."[12] Augustine's interpretation expressed his doctrine of grace, because Peter, and in him the whole church, is built upon Christ alone. This christological interpretation of the rock was very successful. It became the dominant interpretation of the Western church in the Middle Ages. It was not antipapal, because Augustine was a supporter of the Roman church. Most medieval commentators seem to have no idea that Matt. 16:18 could refer to the pope. Thomas Aquinas, whose sympathies for the pope and polemics against the Eastern churches are well known, is one of the few exceptions.[13] Rarely in the Middle Ages[14] but more frequently in the Reformation, the Augustinian interpretation became an argument to refute the pontifical interpretation: Christ, and not the pope, is the rock. Christ wanted to have one rock only; the adherents of the pope have two, says Luther.[15] When the Reformers took over the Augustinian interpretation, they created nothing new but continued the traditional interpretation of the church and gave it an anti-Roman emphasis.

What were the effects of this interpretation? For Augustine it was the result of an exegetical and theological reflection. He read our text "canonically" in the light of the entire New Testament, including Pauline texts like 1 Cor. 3:11; 10:4. For him Christ is the sole basis of the church. One of the reasons for the popularity of

11. Origen, *Comm. on Matt.* 12.10 = GCS Origenes 10.86; Tertullian, *De Praescriptione Haereticorum* 22.4.

12. In *John* 124.5.

13. *Lectura* 1384f. (ed. R. Cai; Turin and Rome: Marietti, 1951) 211.

14. For instance, Tostatus *Op* 21.169f. (see Luz, *Matthäus II*, 478, n. 169).

15. *Luther's Works*, ed. H. T. Lehmann (Philadelphia: Fortress Press, 1958) 32.68–74.

this interpretation may have been that it enabled an easy identification of the Christians with Peter; he is a human being, weak and unstable, not perfect, and he is built upon Christ alone. In Christ the human church and the human, imperfect Christians have their basis. I think that this interpretation was effective because it was a sincere and clear expression of Christian piety.

4. *The Roman interpretation:* Probably in the first part of the third century, the claims of the Roman church to special authority and dignity were legitimated for the first time by Matt. 16:18. The earliest testimonies are unclear. Well known is Tertullian's polemic against the "apostolic Lord," who claims for himself and every church "near to Peter" the authority to bind and loose sins like Peter,[16] but it is disputed whether it really is Bishop Callistus of Rome whom he opposes. Less well known is Origen's polemic against people who think that "the keys of the kingdom of heaven are given to Peter only."[17] Again, unfortunately, we do not know of whom Origen was thinking. The first clear testimony of verse 18 being applied to the bishop of Rome is Stephen (pope, 254–257). Cyprian, who sees Peter as the model of *all* bishops, comments, "An open and manifest stupidity!"[18]

Until the middle of the fifth century we have only a few other testimonies. The famous interpretation of Pope Leo I is interesting because he combines his pontifical interpretation not with the idea of apostolical succession but with a kind of Petrine mysticism. He did not understand himself primarily as successor of Peter, but as his revivification. The living Peter is present in him and in all the Roman bishops. Today it is admitted, even by Roman Catholic research, that this Roman interpretation is an exegetical form of "secondary legitimation."[19] It sought to legitimize the claims to primacy on the part of the Roman church that have other reasons, such as the fact that Rome was the capital, a center of orthodoxy, had the graves of two apostles, and so on. Less known is the fact that during the Middle Ages this Roman interpretation played a

---

16. *De Pudicitia* 21.
17. *Comm. on Matt.* 12.11 = GCS Origenes 10.86.
18. *Epistle* 75.17.
19. H. Döring, "Papsttum," in *Neues Handbuch theologischer Grundbegriffe* (ed. P. Eicher; Munich: Kösel, 1985) 3.318.

very minor role. According to Karlfried Frölich,[20] it was known almost exclusively in certain decretals and is mentioned there only with the goal of supporting papal claims. In the medieval commentaries it is almost nonexistent.

The Roman interpretation was entertained not by the whole Western church but in a more limited sense by its Roman leaders. Its *Sitz im Leben* was and remains the justification of papal claims. It probably owes its final success in the church to the very fact that it was an interpretation articulated by its rulers. An important step toward this success was taken in the sixteenth and the seventeenth centuries. In the controversies with the Protestants, the popes needed this interpretation for their own legitimation against the Protestant use of the hitherto standard Augustinian and Eastern interpretations of the text. Only in the Catholic Reformation of the sixteenth and seventeenth centuries did the Roman interpretation become dominant in Roman Catholic exegesis. The first exegete who propagated it was Cajetan; the most influential book was the defense of the primacy of the pope by Bellarmine.[21] Tragically, Protestantism is the indirect cause for the late victory of this interpretation in the Roman Catholic church. At the first Vatican Council this "late rereading of Scripture"[22] finally prevailed. In 1870 the rock of the Roman pope seemed the only defense against the new attack of the "doors of Hell . . . that rise from day to day with more hatred."[23] The "doors of Hell" were nationalism, Gallicanism, liberal and enlightened ideas, revolutionary tendencies, and the imminent loss of the states of the church to a rising Italy.

The effects of this interpretation in history are so dominant that the other traditional interpretations of our text are almost forgotten today. In the Roman interpretation, the text served as legitimation for an institution. It strengthened and stabilized the papacy against the Roman Empire, against the Eastern patriar-

20. K. Frölich, *Formen der Auslegung von Matthäus 16, 13-18 im lateinischen Mittelalter* (Tübingen: Fotodruck Präzis, 1963) 117.

21. J. Caietanus, *Commentarii in Evangelium* (Venice, 1530) 91; R. Bellarmino, *De Romano Pontifice* (Sedan, 1619) 72–105.

22. W. Kasper, "Dienst an der Einheit und Freiheit der Kirche," in *Dienst an der Einheit* (ed. J. Ratzinger; Düsseldorf: Patmos, 1978) 85.

23. *Pastor Aeternus*, DS[36] no. 3052.

chates, against the emperor in the Middle Ages, against Protestantism, against Modernism, Gallicanism, secularism, and other "doors of Hell."

Openness to New Interpretations and the Question of Truth

How should we evaluate this history of effects? In the hermeneutical reflections of chapter 1, I tried to understand the effects as part of the power of the texts themselves. I compared biblical texts to a source from which water emerges and flows away to new lands and in new directions. I understood interpretation not only as reproduction of old meaning but as production of a new meaning in a new situation out of the old text. I spoke about the power of the texts and interpreted their history of influence as an expression of this power, thus as part of the texts themselves.

Let me now identify a difficulty of this model. If the biblical word moves through history like a river flowing from its source, is it still possible to criticize developments and interpretations that cannot be directly legitimated by the biblical texts but can be understood as their developments and expansions? Is it not possible, and did it not happen, that all new interpretations of the biblical texts that were successful and accepted by the churches were legitimized by means of recourse to the guidance of the Holy Spirit? The idea that the texts have power to create new significance in the course of history is in some way comparable to the classical Roman Catholic doctrine of tradition. According to the constitution on divine revelation of Vatican II, tradition "progresses" and "grows" in the church under the guidance of the Holy Spirit.[24] Is the hermeneutical concept of the history of effects in this respect the same as the Roman Catholic concept of the ongoing and expanding tradition? Cardinal Newman once said that it is not history but "the church's use of history in which the Catholic believes."[25]

24. *De revelatione* 2.8.
25. "Letter to the Duke of Norfolk," quoted by J. A. Burgess, *A History of the Exegesis of Matthew 16:17-19 from 1781 to 1965* (Ann Arbor, Mich.: Edwards, 1976) 87.

No wonder many of my Catholic friends in the working group of the Evangelisch-katholischer Kommentar were not enthusiastic about some of the consequences of my ideas about the history of effects! The question is whether it is possible to reject any of the above-mentioned interpretations of Matt. 16:18 as being contrary to the text or whether we have to admit *every* exegesis—the Augustinian, the Eastern, and the Roman Catholic—as legitimate parts of the tradition of the church, guided by the Holy Spirit. How can the biblical texts become the basis for critique of later historical developments if we accept the idea that they have the legitimate power to create new interpretations and new applications in new situations? Is the freedom given by the texts unlimited? The history of influence seems to dissolve the possibility of truth.

The exegesis of Matt. 16:18 is a real test case for my hermeneutical ideas. Here I have to clarify whether a hermeneutic of the history of effects can escape the awkward position of legitimizing everything that prevailed in history. Because the history of the dominant effects of the Bible is always the history of those who have won and not of those who have lost in the course of history, such a hermeneutic could be nothing but a legitimation of successful historical processes or, even more cynically, nothing but a secondary hermeneutical legitimation of secondary biblical legitimations, which have been used in the history of the church to justify the acts of the rulers of the church or, sometimes, of the rulers of the world.

Is it possible that the original meaning of a text, reconstructed by historical-critical exegesis, can exercise control over new applications? To return to the image of the source: the location of the source determines the general direction of the river emerging from it, but the specific course of the river is not determined merely by the location of the source. Can we say something similar about the original meaning of a text? Are there legitimate and illegitimate applications in the light of its original meaning? And what else beyond it is decisive for the truth of new interpretations?

Some Comments on the Original Meaning of Matthew 16:18[26]

1. My first comment concerns the *synchronic analysis* of our text. Its location is at the end of the section 12:1—16:20, which deals with the conflict between Jesus and the leaders of Israel and the withdrawals of Jesus and his disciples from those leaders (12:15; 14:13; 15:21; 16:4). Here, at the end of the section, Jesus for the first time envisions the future church, a suitable introduction for the next section, 16:21—20:34, which deals with the life and destiny of the church in Israel. We can say that in the macrotext of the Gospel, 16:13-20 is the point where the foundation of the church is considered. That this is connected with Peter, the "first" of the apostles (10:2; cf. 4:18-20), is not by chance. Peter seems to be of special importance to the church.

But there is another side to it. Our pericope is also connected with other pericopes. The revelation of the Son of God by the Father takes up the revelation in 11:25-27 to all the simple ones; the blessing of Peter takes up the blessing of all the disciples in 13:16-17; Peter's confession of the Son of God takes up the confession of all the disciples in 14:33. The power of binding and loosing given to Peter in verse 19 is given to all the disciples in 18:18. So almost nothing is said about Peter that is not said about all the disciples. Especially important is the fact that 16:21-28 seems to be an antithetical and chiastic reprise of 16:13-20. In 16:21-28 Peter plays a negative role. He is no longer called rock, but "scandal." He does not express what is revealed to him by the heavenly Father, but what is according to human thinking and not according to God.

Let me summarize. On the one hand, our pericope has a special position in the macrotext of the Gospel and combines Peter with the foundation of the church. On the other hand, all the cross-references to this text indicate that Peter plays no different role and receives no different blessing from that of all the other disciples.

2. I share the opinion of numerous other scholars that Matt. 16:17-19 is not an old traditional unity, but a composition of single, originally independent units that were probably combined by the

---

26. For detailed argumentation see Luz, *Matthäus II*.

evangelist. They are not a part of an old Easter appearance story—a story containing verses 17-19 would have been a very unusual appearance story! All of the Semitisms in the texts can be explained as biblicisms of a Greek-speaking community or as Semitisms of a bilingual milieu; there is no need therefore to go back to a common Semitic origin of verses 17-19. With many scholars I also share the conviction that verse 17 is a redactional answer of Jesus to the solemn confession of Peter in verse 16 and serves as a transition to the traditional word in verse 18. I am not absolutely certain about this claim. The redactional character of verse 17 is linguistically not very impressive. But the other possibilities are more difficult, and the cross-references to 11:25-27 and other texts are Matthean. If verse 17 is redactional, it appears that it was Matthew's intention to point out the special role of Peter. Apart from the macarism of all the disciples in 13:16, Peter receives a special macarism; and the confession of all the disciples in 14:33 receives a special answer from Jesus when Peter reformulates it in 16:16.

3. Matthew 16:18 contains a traditional word. Peter Lampe's assumption that its origins are in a Greek-speaking community is highly probable.[27] In Greek it is possible to make a wordplay on *petros* (stone) and *petra* (rock). In Aramaic we have the word *kefa* only, which normally means, without any further explanation, "round stone," and only rarely "rock." Simon's Aramaic name *Kefa* (Cephas) is of very early origin (from Jesus?), but the explanation of its Greek translation *Petros* in Matt. 16:18 is a secondary theological explanation.

I think, first, that Matt. 16:18 is of comparatively late date. In postapostolic times—and only then—we have two parallels, based on the symbolism of the church as a temple or building. In Eph. 2:20 the church is a house, built upon apostles and prophets as its foundation. And in Rev. 21:14 the names of the twelve apostles are written on the twelve foundation stones of the heavenly Jerusalem. These words look back to the time of the apostles and describe their role as "foundational" for the church. In the apostolic time, however, the foundational apostles spoke about themselves in

27. P. Lampe, "Das Spiel mit dem Petrus-Namen—Mt 16, 18," *NTS* 25 (1978/79) 227–45.

terms not of a "foundation" for the "church," but in terms of its "pillars" (Gal. 2:9).

Second, I think that Syria, the place of origin of Matthew's Gospel, is a likely place of origin of Matt. 16:18 as well. The reason is twofold: (1) The closest parallel to Peter's role in the Gospel according to Matthew is in the addition to the (for me, Syrian) Johannine Gospel in John 21. John 21:15-17 is a close parallel to Matt. 16:18, and, unlike the Matthean verse, it looks back to the institutional *function* of Peter for the church. In this respect, John 21:15-17 comes closer to the later Roman interpretation of Peter than Matt. 16:18 does.[28] (2) Later, Peter plays an important role in Syria: the Pseudo-Clementine *Homilies* are among the first to interpret Matt. 16:18 as a promise given to Peter personally. In *Hom* 17.18 Peter—and not Paul, which claims are based on a vision only—is the rock as the true guarantor of the tradition of Jesus. In *Hom* 20.23 and *Recognitions* 10.68-71 the *cathedra Petri* is established in Antioch! This corresponds to the later tradition of the church, according to which Peter is the first bishop of Antioch.[29] Therefore I think that Matt. 16:18 originates in Syria in postapostolic times. It belongs to those numerous New Testament texts that look back to the times of the apostles and reflect their unique role in the beginnings of the church, a role that remains of lasting importance.

4. Matthew 16:19a, the word about the keys, could also be a redactional transition between verses 18 and 19bc. Again I have to admit that it is almost impossible to prove that on the basis of language alone. But verse 19a has, like verse 17 and unlike 18 and 19bc, no parallel in the Gospel of John. A transition between verses 18 and 19bc is necessary because Peter is no longer the foundation of the church in verse 19bc but its authoritative teacher, and because the opposition of the church in verse 19bc is no longer the underworld but heaven. The closest, and almost the only, parallel to verse 19a is found in Matthew, namely, 23:13. Here the Pharisees

---

28. R. Brown, *The Gospel According to John* (AB 29B; London: Chapman; Garden City, N.Y.: Doubleday & Co., 1970) 2.1116, says rightly that in John 21:15-17 Peter is not representative of the other disciples.

29. Since Origen, *Hom. on Luke* 6 = GCS Origenes 9.32. See G. Downey, *A History of Antioch in Syria* (Princeton, N.J.: Princeton University Press, 1961) 584-86.

close the kingdom of heaven and allow no one to enter. This—in my opinion, redactional—verse sounds like a contrast to the whole of Matt. 16:19. Thus Peter should do exactly what the Pharisees and scribes do not. The Near Eastern and ancient idea of heaven as a space or a vault with doors fits well with the local Matthean conception of the kingdom of heaven as a place where people enter. Therefore I think that verse 19a is Matthean redaction.

The singular in verse 19bc finally, in my opinion, is secondary to the plural in 18:18. The most important argument is that John 20:23, the only parallel to this word, uses the plural. In the tradition, therefore, all the disciples had the power of binding and loosing. "Binding" and "loosing" mean here primarily Peter's authoritative teaching and interpretation of the law and the commandments of Jesus. This corresponds not only to the mass of rabbinical parallels to this expression but also to 23:13. In the perspective of this interpretation, it is correct to say with exegetes like Gnilka, Mussner, and Pesch[30] that Peter functions as "guarantor of the teaching of Jesus" (Gnilka) and that the perspective of our text for a possible lasting "ministry of Peter" moves in this direction.

I cannot prove that all my exegetical assumptions are correct. Sometimes the basis of my argument is rather fragile. One of its strengths is that all the different elements fit together well. If all this is correct, then Matthew did not eliminate Peter's special task by generalizing or democratizing it in 18:18, but, quite the contrary, he created this special function of Peter by shaping a doublet to Matt. 18:18 in 16:19. He personalizes the authority and the blessing, which in 18:18[31] is given to all disciples, and focuses it on the person of Peter. Therefore one cannot say that Matthew is uninterested in the special function of the "first" apostle Peter and democratizes the tradition, making Peter the representative and type of all the disciples. No! He created this special role for Peter in spite of having had no special tradition, apart from verse 18, for it. This is perfectly understandable for a writer of the postapostolic age, whose interest consists in the uniqueness of the apostles.

30. J. Gnilka, *Das Matthäusevangelium II* (HTKNT I/2; Freiburg, Basel, and Vienna: Herder, 1988) 64; F. Mussner, *Petrus und Paulus—Pole der Einheit* (QD 76; Freiburg, Basel, and Vienna: Herder, 1976) 21; R. Pesch, *Simon-Petrus* (PuP 15; Stuttgart: Hiersemann, 1980) 143f.
31. And in similar texts like Luke 10:5f., 10f., 16.

5. With many other writers, I see the *role of Peter* in Matthew's Gospel to have two aspects that belong together: Peter as a unique figure and Peter as a type of every disciple. To the typological character of Peter belongs his role as "speaker" for the disciples and as Jesus' pupil. He poses questions to Jesus (15:15; 18:21) and gets answers. He makes objections and is corrected by Jesus (16:22f.; 19:27ff.; 26:33f.). Peter's behavior also belongs to his typological function. For Matthew, Peter is a type of the real, not the ideal, disciple. His behavior shows the ambivalence of the reality of the life of a Christian confession and rejection of suffering (16:16-23), denial and repentance (26:33-35, 69-75), courage and failure (14:28-31).

With respect to the uniqueness of Peter, the first matter to state is that the name of Peter is mentioned much more frequently in the Matthean Gospel than that of any other disciple. The comparison with the sons of Zebedee, who were frequently omitted, is striking. We have to ask why *Peter* is presented as the typical disciple. To this we can add 10:2, where Peter is "first" (why not his brother Andrew?), and our text, where Matthew commences his "ecclesiastical section" with Peter. Where are the roots of this uniqueness of Peter in Matthew and also in the other Gospels? Naturally it is possible to mention the special role of Peter in Syria, but this is important only for Matthew, not necessarily for the other Gospels. It seems to me that neither the appearance of the risen Christ first to Peter nor his role as Jewish missionary to the Gentiles in later years was decisive. In all the Synoptic Gospels, that Peter was called as the first disciple by Jesus is more important than anything else. It seems to me that Peter became a central apostolic figure for the early church because of his close association with Jesus. The dominant weight of Peter as the central apostolic figure in the late first and early second centuries corresponds to the central importance of the Jesus-tradition for the early church. Peter became the central foundational figure of the church because *Jesus* is the basis of the church.

For Matthew, the historical uniqueness of Peter and his function as a type of the real disciple belong together. It is easy to understand why. "Church" for Matthew involves discipleship, listening to the words of Jesus, and obeying his commandments. It is in the person of Peter that this basic character of the church becomes visible. "He expresses concretely what is a lasting character of the church according to Matthew: its relationship with and obligation to Jesus."[32] Typological character and unique historical figure belong together.

This has two consequences. The first concerns the concept of apostolic succession. The uniqueness of Peter, which consists of his proximity to Jesus as an eyewitness, cannot be succeeded by anybody. We know that historically there was no succession of the apostles in their apostolic ministry to the whole church in early Christianity, and that there were no apostles after them, only local elders and bishops.[33] The second consequence concerns the concept of a special "ministry of Peter." Peter's typological character, which represents concretely the essence of discipleship for *everybody,* casts serious doubt on any notion of a specialized representation of Peter in only certain members of the church.

Original Meaning, History of Effects, and Truth

What can we say about the truth of different, even contradictory, interpretations of a text in relation to its original meaning? Are they all legitimate, insofar as every branch of the tree of the history of effects that grew out of the root—the text itself—is a legitimate expression of its power?

A "liberal" conclusion. The first remark to be made is that none of the four traditional types of interpretation corresponds exactly to the Matthean text. In each interpretation we can detect new historical experiences and concerns that the interpretations answered. In some way it is the variety of interpretations that corresponds to the message of the New Testament, insofar as new applications and new forms of Christian identity belong to the biblical texts. In

---

32. P. Hoffman, "Der Petrus-Primat im Matthäusevangelium," in *Neues Testament und Kirche* (Festschrift for R. Schnackenburg; ed. J. Gnilka; Freiburg, Basel, and Vienna: Herder, 1974) 110.

33. The classic book to show this is O. Cullmann, *Peter: Disciple, Apostle, Martyr,* trans. F. V. Filsen (Rev. ed., London: SCM, 1962) 220ff.

the very moment in which one single interpretation is established as the sole interpretation and is used to suppress the others, an essential element of the Bible's spirit of freedom is lost. This is particularly dangerous when such all interpretation becomes the official interpretation of a church. It is important that all the rich and different experiences of faith that were condensed in the various interpretations become visible in our own attempts at interpretation.

Correspondence with the original meaning.   We have to go farther than this very general statement. Let us look first at the correspondence between the various interpretations and the biblical text. The degree of proximity of each type of interpretation of our text to the Bible and to the Matthean text varies. The typological interpretation takes up a basic element of Matthew and the whole Gospel tradition— namely, the character of the disciples as figures with whom the readers can identify. It takes seriously the fact that Matthew did not say anything in our text about Peter that he did not say about all the disciples. The Eastern interpretation holds the Matthean idea that Peter's proximity to *Jesus* makes him the guarantor of the tradition of Jesus and through this the rock of the church. Both of these interpretations are comparatively close to the original meaning of the text, especially the Eastern interpretation, which takes up a basic interest of Matthew.

The distance between the other two interpretations and the original meaning is greater. The Augustinian interpretation is rather far from the original meaning of our text, but it does take seriously the message of the entire New Testament that Jesus Christ is the sole foundation of the church. Its basis is not primarily our text, but the New Testament message as a whole. A Pauline text (1 Cor. 3:11) shaped this interpretation. The Augustinian interpretation is a kind of canonical interpretation of our text, and it is a reminder that such an attempt is necessary. Our interpretation today must be guided by the whole or the center of the biblical message, not only by the original meaning of each single biblical text.[34]

34. Unlike B. Childs, *The New Testament as Canon: An Introduction* (Minneapolis: Fortress Press, 1985) 35–44, for me, the "canonical" dimension belongs to the (applicative) understanding and not to the historical and descriptive "explanation" of texts, that is, not to the historical "introduction" into the Bible, where it is anachronistic.

The Roman interpretation takes seriously the promise Jesus gave to Peter personally. It does not consider, however, that the unique apostle Peter, as the rock of the church, excludes all other rocks after him, as is clear from Matthew's metaphors: the rock does not grow when the house is going to be constructed. The walls of a house are built upon a foundation; but the foundation does not develop further. This interpretation also fails to consider the typological character of Peter, who is a model for *all* Christians. The transformation of the authority given to Peter into a special institution, a predominantly juridical primacy, and its separation from the authority given to every Christian, make the Roman interpretation the most innovative of all the different interpretations. I think that no other interpretation is so far from the New Testament text as this one.

But does that make it wrong? Does it not belong to the freedom given by the Spirit that new experiences, new historical situations, and new demands create not only new interpretations but also new institutions? Is it really illegitimate to go so far beyond the New Testament as the institution of the Roman pope does? Is not that also a possibility offered by the New Testament, at least as long as it does not claim to be the only possibility? And is it not possible and, in some ways, even necessary to admit that this institution, secondarily and exegetically incorrectly legitimized by Matt. 16:18, has also served the "ministry of Peter," insofar as it did remind the church of its only foundation, namely, the tradition, the history, and the message of Jesus? And is it not also true that this institution, at least sometimes, has served this ministry better than other ecclesiastical institutions and organizations? These reflections show the need of a second, functional criterion besides the criterion of correspondence to the biblical context. In order to judge the truth of a new interpretation of a biblical text, we have to ask what such an interpretation provokes and effects in its own time.

A functional criterion cannot be merely formal. If this were the case, then the historical or political success of an interpretation in the course of history would be decisive for the truth; then the interpretations of the winners and rulers in history would always be "true." Instead, this criterion—as a theological criterion—cannot be established independently from the history of Jesus, to which it must correspond. Looking at single texts, we could ask whether the "fruit" of an interpretation corresponds to its intentions. But this inquiry is insufficient, because we need once again a "canonical" criterion that considers the intentions of the New Testament as a whole. I propose to take love as the center of what the history of Jesus wanted to provoke. My formulation of the second criterion is this: does an interpretation or an actualization of a text bring forward love? I will postpone the general discussion of this criterion for the moment[35] and try to apply it to our text and its interpretations.

It is easy to give a positive answer for the Augustinian interpretation. It is an expression of the reliability of Christ, who is a rock for all unreliable, weak, and unstable Christians, like Peter. This interpretation conveys something of God's unshakable love for human beings. As for the Eastern interpretation of our text, I think the answer depends on how "faith" was understood. I would like to give a negative answer in situations where the faith of the church was "petrified" into a rigid system of doctrines that had to be accepted by the faithful in total heteronomy. This is not a foundation that corresponds to the spirit of love. But there were other situations in the history of the church where faithfulness to the "foundation" of the Christian confession was the basis not only of Christian identity but also of limitless love.

As for the pontifical interpretation, I would like to admit for a moment that even a monarchical head of the church could be one (not the only) legitimate use of the freedom offered by the New Testament for construing a church. How should such a monarchical institution function in the light of Matt. 16:18? First, it must serve the "ministry of Peter." That is, like Peter it must also submit itself to the authority of the mission and teaching of Jesus. Its own authority cannot have such ultimacy that it is above the criticism from that which it wants to serve. It cannot be an infallible authority without the possibility of admitting its own errors in the light of the mission and teaching of Jesus. I think that infallibility tends to destroy what I would call the ministerial character necessary for

35. See pp. 91–96 in this book.

such an institution. Second, if a church has a head that is the focus of the whole church, this arrangement is viable only if this head symbolizes what all Christians are and nothing more than that. A pope, seen in the light of our text and of Matthean theology, can be a visible representation of the whole church, but not its ruler. The view of the pope as a nonabsolute and truly representative head of the church could be a new interpretation of Matt. 16:18 in the spirit of love. This is how I would apply the functional criterion to the Roman interpretation of our text.

Is this Roman interpretation therefore a legitimate possibility? When we apply the functional criterion, the answer need not be no. The memory of a pope like John XXIII, who was visibly representing the gifts, the authenticity, and the fidelity of the church to Jesus, and who was becoming more and more the representative of the hopes of the whole church for visible unity, not just its Roman Catholic part, can engender hopes. But his time is gone now. It is also a lesson of history that an affirmative answer is not easy. A papacy that is far from corresponding to the history of Jesus Christ and therefore is dependent on secondary biblical legitimations for its dominant position carries its own history as a heavy burden.

FIVE

THE HISTORY OF EFFECTS AND THE QUESTION OF TRUTH

Let me first recapitulate the main points of the first chapters.

1. What does it mean to understand a biblical text today? It does not mean to gain an abstract, timeless knowledge of a theological truth. Nor does it mean only to reconstruct its original meaning or situation detached from us. But it does mean, beyond this, to incorporate the text into one's own life and to discover its new meaning in and for one's own situation. It includes its own application.

2. What is the significance of the history of effects of the biblical texts? It shows us that the biblical texts are like a source. Its waters emerge from one point but flow away from it into new directions. Like water whose flow is shaped by the terrain in a new land, the texts take on new meanings in new situations. The history of effects of the biblical texts also shows us that we are not separated from them but live in the stream that they created.

3. What is the significance of the original meaning of the biblical texts? How can the source be responsible for the directions the stream takes afterward? Here we are still left with an open question.

Our model of the text as a power creating new meanings in history runs into difficulties when we want to decide what are legitimate and illegitimate developments stimulated by biblical texts. For example, the original meaning of Matt. 16:18 in itself had no strength to prohibit its application to the papacy, because between the original meaning and our interpretation were a lot of new situations, challenges, and experiences that could not be anticipated by the text. A text understood as a productive power for new meanings in new situations cannot be simply a criterion of truth, because truth itself does not and cannot remain the same in the course of history. Therefore the principle of the history of effects seems to render impossible an authoritative function of its original meaning.[1] This causes a great problem, especially for Protestants, because their basic principle, "the Scripture alone," seems to be a fiction. Scripture is never "alone"; it belongs to its rich history of effects, as the stem of a tree belongs to its branches. How is it possible to differentiate between legitimate and illegitimate branches? This leads us to the first and most fundamental question of this chapter: *How do we distinguish false from true interpretations of Scripture?* Is it possible to maintain the critical function of the Scripture when we maintain that every understanding means new understanding?

There is yet a second problem: What kind of normative function does the original meaning of a text have? I started this book with the problems of the historical-critical method. We have seen how the traditional "literal" meaning of Scripture was replaced in the Enlightenment by the "original," "historical" meaning. Let me recall some limitations of the historical approach.

1. Historical interpretations are always reconstructions that are hypothetical and disputed among scholars. Should and can our historical hypotheses decide on matters of truth? How can we be sure that it is *the* and not *our* meaning of a text that we want to

---

1. This principle is similar in the hermeneutics of liberation theology and feminist criticism. C. Boff, *Theology and Praxis*, trans. R. Barr (Maryknoll, N.Y.: Orbis, 1987) 146–50, proposes a hermeneutical model based on the correspondence of relationships, e.g., between Scripture and our interpretation, and the political context then and now. E. Schüssler Fiorenza, *Bread Not Stone: The Challenge of Feminist Biblical Interpretation* (Boston: Beacon Press, 1984) 8–15, distinguishes between the Bible as an archetype and the Bible as a prototype for a community. I understand my own hermeneutical reflections as a parallel attempt, although my context is not so much the liberation movements but the situation of European academic theologians and students of theology. It involves finding one's way between the normative authority of the tradition and the complete loss of our history. We have to regain a concept of *living* authority!

make authoritative? There remains an element of subjectivity in historical interpretation.

2. Historical reconstructions *atomize* the biblical truth and dissolve it into the voices of Paul, James, Jesus, Q, and Matthew; into what Paul said to the Corinthians and later said to the Romans, and what he said in a good moment or what he said in a bad moment of his life. What kind of voices in Scripture shall we prefer? There is no limit to the subjectivity of the interpreter! The traditional-canonical meaning of Scripture, regulated by the faith of the church or by the Reformation principle of the centrality of Scripture, seems to be replaced by the individual choice of theologians among a variety of different biblical witnesses. The Bible becomes a kind of self-service supermarket through historical criticism.

3. Behind this is the problem that historical reconstructions that try to take the texts back to their original situations and their first listeners or readers prevent the texts from speaking beyond their original situations. Every historical situation is unique, and a text that belongs to a situation in the past is per se separated from me, whose life and situation are different.

What is the significance of the original meaning of a text, and what is the significance of the historical-critical method? How is it possible that history can offer fundamental truths for the present? This is the second question to be answered.

The Example of the Tares

The parable of the tares (Matt. 13:24-30, 36-43) and its history of interpretation will sharpen and clarify the problems. I will not enter into a lengthy exegetical discussion but will give you my own views.[2] The parable (vv. 24-30) and its interpretation (vv. 37-43) are separated in the Gospel. The interpretation, in my opinion, is entirely Matthean in language and thought. The parable takes the

---

2. For a detailed discussion, see U. Luz, *Das Evangelium nach Matthäus II (Mt 8–17)* (EKKNT I/2; Neukirchen-Vluyn: Neukirchener; Zurich: Benziger, 1990) 320–26, 337–48.

place of the Markan parable of the seed growing secretly (Mark 4:26-29). One of its characteristics is the many allusions and connections in words and motives to this Markan parable. Formally it is a strange story. More than half of it consists of the farmer's lengthy discourse, in which he tells what will happen later at harvesttime. It is strange that the sower is also called the master of the house, and his servants are distinguished from the harvesters. This arrangement fits well with the allegorical interpretation of verses 37-43, but it does not make a good parable, which requires economy of persons and times.

Opinions about the origin and development of the parable are divided.

1. Does it go back to Jesus? Scholars who think that Jesus actually spoke this parable have to change and shorten the present wording considerably. This is highly arbitrary, and the results of the varied attempts are far from being generally accepted. I renounce this attempt and admit that we know nothing about a possible original parable formulated by Jesus.

2. There remains the pre-Matthean church, from which the evangelist has taken the parable. There are two main possibilities in reconstructing it. The first is the idea that the parable was used in the church to clarify the position of the followers of Jesus toward unbelieving Israel. Then it functioned as a warning not to separate prematurely from the unbelieving part of Israel. In this case it was later assimilated to Mark 4:26-29 in order to reinterpret and correct it. The other possibility is to regard the allusions to Mark 4:26-29 as part of the original version. Then the parable was formulated from the beginning as an allegory that critically reinterpreted the parable of the seed growing secretly in the light of new experiences. The point of departure then was the experience of evil in the church. After the sower has sown the seed, he is going to sleep. But when he does so, the seed does not grow properly because the enemy comes and sows the bad seed, which is also growing. The parable then is a critical reformulation of Mark 4:26-29, which became necessary because the church was not the pure field of the good sower alone. Its interest, according to this view, was not the relation of the church to Israel but the internal situation of the church. I prefer this second explanation, but I am not certain of it. Both approaches

assume that an experience in a concrete situation led to the formulation or reformulation of the story.

3. In Matthew's interpretation (13:37-43) the text is an allegory with a parenetical scope. Matthew wants to warn his church to see to it that they do not belong to the tares, the lawless scandals, that the Son of man will throw into the fire at the final judgment. Matthew speaks to a situation in which the Christians are getting tired and ethically lax. At the same time, he integrates his own universalistic horizon into the interpretation of the parable. The kingdom of the Son of man is the world, toward which the mission of the disciples is now directed. Matthew's situation is the beginning of his church's mission to the Gentiles. That means that Matthew has again adapted the traditional parable to his own situation; he included his own universalistic horizon and applied the parable parenetically as a warning.

4. Let us turn to the later history of interpretation. One crucial problem to be solved with the help of this parable was the question of the purity of the church. It was important in the debates with the adherents of Novatianus and Donatus. The parable was used to explain why good and bad people live together in the church. It was again important in the Reformation in the debates with the Anabaptists and other so-called enthusiasts. Particularly in post-Reformation theology the text became a basic proof text for the understanding of the church as a "mixed body" of good and bad people. Here our text got the dignity of a basic ecclesiological text. As such, it remained important as a theological and ideological justification of European state churches or folk churches and in their understandings of church discipline.

Our text was used also in the debates about heresies. It explained why the true Christians sometimes had to tolerate heretics in the church. The farmer's answer in verses 29-30 was very important. He said, "Let both grow together, so that you don't uproot the wheat along with the tares." The standard application, found in many churches, was as follows: only when there is danger to the wheat should the tares be allowed to grow, but when there is no danger to the wheat, the tares should be removed. That meant that where the orthodox Christians were in a majority, they should eliminate the heretics;[3] where they lived as a minority, they must live together with and ask for tolerance from the heretical majority. Only under the influence of humanism and the Enlightenment was our text used to promote tolerance as a principle.[4]

What can we learn from this text?

1. The original meaning of the text as a parable of the historical Jesus cannot be a criterion for new applications in this case. Matthew 13:24-30 belongs to those texts whose original meaning is hardly discernible, be it in the teaching of Jesus or in the pre-Matthean church. Matthew's interpretation is the earliest clearly discernible interpretation.

2. Our text is a good example of the freedom of interpretation that was already present in New Testament times, especially if it is an adaption of Mark 4:26-29.

3. For Matthew's reinterpretation, three factors were important: (*a*) the traditional story; (*b*) Matthew's own situation, mainly the worldwide mission to the Gentiles and the need for exhortation and parenesis; (*c*) his understanding of the risen Lord. To a large extent his reinterpretation conforms to his Christology: Christ is the exalted Lord of the world for Matthew. Christ gives his church a missionary task for the world. The church is understood as the group of disciples whose obedience will be judged by the Son of man when he judges the world.

4. In the later applications, the same model of reinterpretation was repeated. New situations necessitated new emphases. The traditional story always functioned as the matrix for new interpretations. The new interpretations always corresponded to the doctrine of the church and to its understanding of the risen Christ. The process of interpretation is not fundamentally but only gradually different in the progression from the oral text to the written text and finally to the canonical written text. The matrix became more stable as the text was interpreted. But the freedom of interpretation remained, although it became limited, because not only the Matthean interpretation (vv. 37-43) but also the traditional interpretations of the church were added to the matrix of the text

---

3. The text could thus be used to justify the inquisition.

4. See R. H. Bainton, "Religious Liberty and the Parable of the Tares," in idem, *Collected Papers in Church History I* (Boston: Beacon Press, 1962) 95–121.

and had to be considered in new interpretations. But, as a whole, our parable is an excellent example of how a biblical text remained open for new meanings and new applications in new situations, and how it contained a plurality of potential applications.

5. For all the reinterpretations in and after the New Testament, we can say that every new interpretation was an application at the same time. There was no interpretation of the text that was not at the same time an interpretation of the situation of the author's own church or an answer to its problems. And there was no interpretation that was not guided by the fundamentals of the understanding of Christ held by the interpreters, whether it be the incarnation of the Son of God, the dogma of the church, or the justifying Christ.

What about the truth of all these reinterpretations? I feel that not every application and new interpretation of this text is "true." Some interpretations in the history of effects strike us spontaneously as wrong. We feel this not only because they are wrong for us, because we live in another time, but also because they were wrong in their own time. The legitimation of an inquisition or the persecution of heretics in a minority situation are examples of such wrong interpretations. In such cases, it is difficult to believe that they were flowers on the rich tree of effective history. But how is one to argue about the truth or falsity of these new applications?

Naturally one can argue about correspondence with the text. One can say that verse 29 (in order that you don't uproot the wheat along with the tares) is abused in an interpretation that legitimates action against heretics, because this sentence is not meant conditionally but absolutely. It forbids the disciples' uprooting the tares without restriction. But this argument is of limited value. Every text has to be interpreted in the light of the New Testament message as a whole. It was always easy to find other New Testament references that seemed to sanction the inquisition and similar practices and to interpret our text in harmony with them. We have to look for more fundamental criteria to decide between what is a true and a false interpretation. These criteria must take into account the New Testament as a whole.[5]

5. Here I have to disagree with H. G. Gadamer, who renounces criteria, because the effective power of the tradition precedes the interpreting subject. Yes,

In the following reflections I will propose two criteria. One is the *correspondence with the essentials of the history of Jesus*. It has to do with the unique past that is essential for Christian faith. The other is a functional one and refers to *the effects or fruits of interpretations* in history or today. With regard to content, I will propose that it is *love*. We have to ask: (1) Does a new application correspond with the fundamentals of the history of Jesus? (2) Are the fruits of the texts an expression of love? When we reflect on the first criterion, we will have to speak about the significance of the original meaning and of the historical-critical method as well.

The Criterion of Correspondence and the History of Jesus

Christianity is a product of the unique history of Jesus and has its legitimacy through this history alone. Therefore in Christianity something like correspondence with the fundamental past of the history of Jesus has always been a criterion of truth. But what "history" means has changed, especially through the Enlightenment. Let us first look back to the New Testament and then to the epoch before the Enlightenment.

For Matthew, the guideline of truth in his interpretation of the parable was not simply Jesus but the exalted Lord Jesus, present in the church as "Immanuel" always, until the end of the world (28:20; cf. 1:23). This Jesus carries the marks of Matthew's theology. He is the Son of man whose field is the whole world. In Matthew, more than in any other Gospel, Jesus is the teacher of the Father's will. This is the reason Matthew's interpretation of the parable of the tares had such a strong parenetical accent. Nevertheless, Matthew's exalted Lord is not his theological creation. Quite the opposite. It is Jesus, not an anonymous Holy Spirit, who is present

---

but this does not make superfluous a critical attitude on the part of the interpreting subject. How else could we avoid a preponderance of the tradition, which again leads its recipients into sheer heteronomy? How else could we avoid having interpreters become victims of the respective *Zeitgeist* and its attitude to the tradition? How could we avoid a mere traditionalism? The imposing character of a tradition is no guarantor of its truth, because there are many and contradicting traditions.

in his church.[6] To be the church today means, for Matthew, to follow Jesus' way of life and to be his pupil. Matthew's gospel for his own time is nothing other than Jesus' message of the kingdom. Decisive in the last judgment is obedience to his commandments. That is why, for Matthew, every single command of Jesus is important.

Matthew's tendency to correspond to the way and teaching of Jesus is evident. The same is true for Luke, who narrates the history of Jesus exactly as he heard it from witnesses and read it in his sources. But his intention cannot have been merely historical, namely, to make the "mere" history of Jesus the basis of Christian truth. His writing of the Book of Acts, and particularly his concept of the Holy Spirit, prevent such an idea. The Lukan theology of the Spirit has many hermeneutical implications and stands for the fact that God's history with the world does not end with Jesus. It is a continuing history that asks for reinterpretation and new application.[7] Similar observations could be made about Markan, Pauline, or Johannine theology, although in John Jesus is seen more with the eyes of faith than in the first and the third Gospels.

In a similar way, Jesus—the living Jesus of faith and not merely the historical person—was the matrix in the traditional ecclesiastical hermeneutic. For the Eastern Orthodox tradition, the criterion was the incarnated Christ. In the Western tradition, however, it was Christ as he was confessed in the Creed and taught in the doctrines of the church. For the Reformers, it was "the history of Christ for us," or Jesus Christ, who justified the sinner, and not the mere history of Jesus "painted on a wall."[8] In the time of the ancient church and of the Reformation, the history of Jesus was not only a history that antedated its recipients, a unique and unchangeable event of the past, but it was also an event in which the recipients

---

6. See G. Bornkamm's fundamental essay "The Risen Lord and the Earthly Jesus," in *The Future of Our Religious Past*, trans. C. E. Carlston and R. P. Scharlemann (ed. J. M. Robinson; New York: Harper & Row, 1971) 203–29.

7. See the application of Jesus' call to renounce possessions in Acts 20:35, or the reinterpretation of Jesus' attitude toward the law in the mission to the Gentiles in Acts 10.

8. M. Luther, "Predigten des Jahres 1529," *M. Luther Werke: Kritische Gesamtausgabe* (Weimar) 29.262. See also *Luther's Works*, ed. and trans. J. Pelikan (St. Louis: Concordia, 1972) 12.338.

participated. For Christians, it was a history that gave them an identity, because it preceded their identity. Thus for the church fathers and the Reformers, to "understand" a biblical text was primarily an act of faith and not merely an act of reason or criticism.

What has changed as a result of the Enlightenment in our modern historical consciousness? How can we take over and adapt what our predecessors meant by the living history of Jesus, the incarnated Christ, or the humanity of Jesus? We realize that the formulations of the "criterion of correspondence" were not the same either for the different biblical authors or later in the history of the church. We interpret these criteria again historically and try to understand why John, Matthew, or Paul had to formulate their vision of Jesus Christ as they did, or why Origen, Athanasius, or Luther had to speak in their situations about the Logos, the incarnate Christ, or about justification by faith alone. We realize that these criteria were true not only because they corresponded to the essentials of the history of Jesus but also because they were meaningful for their time and met the needs of the people then. We realize that both the biblical texts and the criterion for their truth are, to speak with José Míguez Bonino,[9] neither beyond history nor an abstract heavenly truth. We also realize that formulations and criteria of truth are nothing but interpretation and application— not only of one biblical text but of the Bible as a whole. The criteria, too, belong to the effective history of the Bible. This is what historical criticism teaches us.

This teaching creates problems for us. With what history of Jesus shall we correspond? With Matthew's? Or with John's? With the shapers of the canon? And if we look at the ongoing history of the church, we can continue to ask: Should we correspond with Luther's vision of the history of Jesus? With Calvin's? Or with the so-called real history of Jesus as reconstructed by modern exegetes (as our liberal fathers did)?

We have the choice. Historical criticism seems to condemn us to our subjectivity. We cannot simply achieve a "fusion" of horizons so that history becomes true for us, as Gadamer thinks.[10] Rather

---

9. J. Míguez Bonino, *Doing Theology in a Revolutionary Situation* (Philadelphia: Fortress Press, 1975) 88.

10. See Gadamer, *Truth and Method*, trans. J. Weisenheimer and D. G. Marshall (New York: Crossroad, 1982) 273.

we have to make decisions about this history and its different possible horizons.[11] And for this we have to study it as exactly as we can, and only then, in a second step, we have to decide personally which view of the history of Jesus seems most meaningful to us. The history of Christian hermeneutics has always contained a subjective and personal factor in the correspondence with the fundamentals of the history of Jesus, but we, through our modern historical consciousness, know about it and cannot escape this knowledge.

The result of this reflection seems to be a dilemma. As soon as we exclude the subjective, personal element from the fundamentals of the history of Jesus, this history becomes distant, abstract, and cannot affect our lives anymore. But when we try to avoid this and conscientiously choose our view of the fundamentals of the history of Jesus, the criterion of correspondence is nothing more than our personal criterion. Therefore our modern historical consciousness seems to weaken the idea that the history of Jesus is an objective, normative criterion.

At this point we have to ask about the contribution of historical criticism to the question of truth. Is it a purely negative contribution?

The Value of the Historical-Critical Method

I think that our way of looking historically and critically at the history of Jesus and its history of effects has many benefits. In my opinion, it does not weaken the criterion of correspondence but shows how it should be used. It does not dissolve the authority of the history of Jesus but shows what its true character is. Let me mention a few points.

The nonimposing character of God and human freedom. Historical criticism shows that God's truth is given to us as history and nothing

11. I think that we need not only an "effective-historical consciousness" (*Truth and Method* 325), but also a "historical consciousness," which relativizes and questions our "effective-historical consciousness" and makes its historical and situational circumstances clear. They are complementary: effective-historical consciousness prevents us from losing the experience of history; historical consciousness prevents us from absolutizing history and tradition.

more. All historical events are contingent, ambiguous, accidental, and hypothetical from our perspective. Historical events are per se not eternal truths that impose themselves on all rational people. God—in this history—is not demonstrable, as scholastic theology, orthodoxy, and fundamentalism seem to think, so that the uniqueness of the history of Jesus could become evident. The human history of Jesus—not of a divinized Jesus—does not impose itself but invites one to a dialogue about truth; and a dialogue includes the possibility of rejection. History is always ambiguous[12] and gives human listeners room for their own decisions. A God who has become human has lost his unambiguous character. Hans Weder, who emphasizes this point, speaks excellently about the "violability" of divine truth in historical shape and sees here an analogy to incarnation.[13] Historical criticism therefore prevents the history of Jesus from being a formal, absolute authority. It presents it as a piece of human history that might impress us but that allows us to formulate our questions.

The accessibility of God in history.   One of the hotly debated questions is whether only believers can understand biblical texts and whether Christian faith is a presupposition for understanding them. For fundamentalists this is so; and most of the authors of the New Testament seem to lean toward this position.[14] I think that historical criticism opens new perspectives at this point. It enables a differentiation between explaining and understanding, between the reconstruction of the meaning of the text and the application of its significance in life. Historical-critical explanation does not presuppose faith. It is not, in a direct way, the work of the Holy Spirit. It presupposes only the persistent intention of the interpreter to allow these texts to tell their own stories. It makes it possible for the non-Christian, also for the non-Christian inside us, to enter into a dialogue with the texts. A historical-critical exegete does not

12. See D. Tracy, *Plurality and Ambiguity* (San Francisco: Harper & Row, 1987) 66–70.

13. H. Weder, *Neutestamentliche* (*Hermeneutik*; Zürich: Theologischer Verlag Zürich, 1986) 393.

14. See Mark's theology of discipleship as the place of understanding; Matthew's link between obedience and understanding; John's affinity between "believing" (*pisteuein*) and "knowing" (*ginōskein*).

have to decide whether Paul actually speaks about God when he uses the word *God*. The only thing he or she has to do is to acknowledge that Paul intends to speak about God. Historical-critical exegesis thus offers nonbelievers the opportunity to enter into a dialogue with the texts. It makes God, in his historical shape, accessible.

The nonabsolute character of human theology. Historical criticism prevents us from absolutizing our own authority. It teaches us to differentiate between historical meanings and our new interpretations, between the otherness of history and the contingency of a new application. We learn to differentiate between Jesus and his interpreters in the Bible and in the history of its interpretation.[15] Historical criticism shows us how, in all epochs, criteria and dogmas were nothing other than interpretations with their own contingencies, conditioned by historical, social, and psychological circumstances. The different interpretations of Matt. 16:18 provide a good example. Thus it is impossible that an interpreter's standpoint or a biblical text can become the ultimate authority. Beyond that, historical criticism shows how often in the history of Christianity, from the biblical times until today, interpreters and churches have absolutized their own theological points by means of what they understood to be the history of Jesus. The self-absolutizing of the Corinthian parties in 1 Cor. 1:18—3:4 is one biblical example. This self-absolutizing has happened many times by means of dogma, preaching, and theology. Again and again Christian interpreters have used "God" or "Jesus Christ" as an instrument to absolutize their own human standpoint and to defend their own interests. Because this has happened so often, Christianity desperately needs the ideology-critical potential of historical criticism.

15. I agree with K. Berger's (*Hermeneutik des Neuen Testaments* [Gütersloh: G. Mohn, 1988] 108–23) separation of explanation and application, which is necessary for the sake of both the integrity of the text and human freedom in application. Unlike him, I would not subsume "understanding" under "explaining" (ibid., 146f.), because I would emphasize more strongly the defective and alienated character of a "mere" abstract explanation. For me, understanding is possible only today and for today, and it includes either (affirmatively) application or (negatively) rejection or criticism of a text, i.e., an element of personal decision.

The biblical potential for freedom and different forms of Christian identity.
Historical criticism reminds us of the potential of freedom and of
different forms of identities that are possible on the basis of the
history of Jesus. Jesus Christ enables not one Christian identity but
many, for example, yours and mine. Historical criticism clarifies
the fact that one text produced quite different interpretations and
applications. It opens the history of Jesus and shows how it functioned as not only a criterion and measure, but also as creative
power and the potential of freedom. Again I can refer to the history
of application of Matt. 16:17f. The variety of applications and interpretations is a fruit of one text. Historical criticism reminds us
that the history of Jesus is not a defined truth. It is a starting point
of a way on which other people have gone before us and on which
finally we have to go. Its first stages are documented in the New
Testament itself. Historical criticism helps us to see that the history
of Jesus and the texts witnessing to it give a direction to our applications but do not regulate them in an absolute sense. Historical
criticism shows how other people have dealt with biblical texts
and thus gives us analogies and examples for finding our way
with these same texts. It indirectly tells us that we have to find
our own way with the texts, and that there is no other way to
understand them.

The invitation to dialogue.   Historical criticism opens the possibility
of a dialogue. Whatever view of the history of Jesus I choose, it
must be submitted to a dialogue with the texts themselves and
with other people's views of these texts. Nobody possesses historical truths. All our historical results are hypothetical and need
verifications and corrections. And all our applications are *our* applications, taken at our own risk and responsibility. They too need
corrections and dialogue. Thus the postulate of the correspondence
with the essentials of the history of Jesus leads to a dialogue. In
this dialogue about Jesus, every participant has to presuppose that
he or she could be biased and one-sided and that the partner's
ideas could be closer to the truth than one's own. What is rational
is not the divine truth in itself, as the Enlightenment supposed,
but our dialogue about it. The philosopher Jürgen Habermas pos-
tulated the consensus resulting from rational discourse as the basis

for communal action.[16] This kind of consensus must be taken as such a basis, because the ideal situation for communication—with no suppression of knowledge, but with equality and rationality—can only be anticipated. Truth is not reached by means of dialogue, but truth is *in* the dialogue, or one might say, truth *is* the dialogue. All this discussion might seem regrettable for those who are looking for absolute truth. Are my proposals just one of the destructive consequences of the Enlightenment and its destruction of absolute truth? For me they have positive consequences. Such a view of correspondence with the fundamentals of the history of Jesus is no basis for excluding and condemning others who have different but also tentative and provisional ideas about this history. This approach does not lead to relativity but prevents the history of Jesus from functioning as a criterion of truth in a way that contradicts this history itself.

Dialogue as a Way between Relativity and Absolute Truth

How can such an understanding of the history of Jesus function as a criterion for the search for truth? I want to reply with a biblical reminiscence. Paul had to dispute with the pneumatics in Corinth, who absolutized their own spiritual gifts. In 1 Cor. 12:3 he opened the discussion and formulated a criterion for the true pneumatic: "No one speaking by the Spirit of God, says: 'Let Jesus be cursed!' and no one can say 'Jesus is the Lord' except by the Holy Spirit." This is the Pauline way of formulating our criterion of correspondence. How did it function? Naturally nobody in the Corinthian church cursed Jesus. Quite the contrary! Everybody in the Corinthian church joined this basic acclamation of the Lord Jesus, which took place in the common worship. The criterion functioned not as an exclusivist criterion but as an *inclusivist* one. It told the Corinthian glossolalists and charismatics that they were nothing special and that everybody for whom Jesus is the Lord is a pneumatic

16. J. Habermas, "Vorbereitende Bemerkungen zu einer Theorie der kommunikativen Kompetenz," in J. Habermas and L. Lohmann, *Theorie der Gesellschaft oder Sozialtechnologie: Was leistet die Systemforschung?* (Frankfurt: Suhrkamp, 1971) 122, 136–40.

and a member of the body of Christ. This criterion led the Corinthian pneumatics into dialogue, mutual dependence, and an edifying process of love.

This is important for us. I do not think that "correspondence with the history of Jesus" can function today primarily as an exclusive criterion. For many centuries the correct interpretation of the history of Jesus was used by churches as a criterion that would exclude dissenters and heretics. Even today the reference to the history of Jesus is used as an excluding criterion within the churches and toward Jews, members of other religions, and atheists. I think it very important that a historical approach to the history of Jesus prohibits every kind of divinization of our views about him. To change Lessing's old dictum: A historical truth is no basis for a dogma. To modify Hans Weder: The violability of God in history and the humanity of the incarnate God prohibits its abuse as an exclusivist criterion. Or, to paraphrase John 14:6: The history of Jesus is a way and enables a way. It is a criterion not in the sense of limiting the truth but in the sense of making the search for it possible. It is the point from which Christians in their search for truth depart and to which they return. In this way, I think, exegesis and study of the history of influence of the Bible are central theological disciplines, precisely because they are not dogmatic in a narrow sense of the word and do not lead to *the* truth but to Matthew's truth or to Origen's truth and thus help us on the way toward our own truth.

In this way, our criterion corresponds to the history of Jesus. For centuries the history of Jesus was used as raw material for a doctrine. That means that the history of Jesus Christ had been replaced by a doctrine about this history. But it is only possible to define a doctrine. With the help of doctrinal criteria it is possible to excommunicate. Doctrinal criteria have a definitional character. A history, however, cannot be defined but only interpreted. The history of Jesus, made accessible to everybody by means of historical criticism, can be narrated. It functions as a model. It invites communication. Theology with such a basis cannot be simply normative or prescriptive. Rather, when Jesus Christ is truth in the sense of a way, theology can be compared to a map. A map describes ways, but it is not merely descriptive. A map also shows which ways lead to a specific place and which ways lead nowhere. A map thus enables us to find our own way. But it does not take away from me the responsibility for deciding the destination of my way and for choosing my own way among the different available ways. And the possession of a map does not guarantee me that I am on the right track. For this, a lot of attention and a lot of communication with other hikers is necessary.

Christian truth is not a definition but a way that corresponds with the model of the history of Jesus and is made possible through his history. Jesus Christ is not a defined truth but a starting point and a goal. Does that mean relativity? Does that mean we must renounce a clear and firm Christian identity? Ways are not good for anything if people do not walk on them. When I am walking by myself on a way that is unknown to me, I am interested in other people's experiences of travel on the way. I know that not "all roads lead to Rome," as a German proverb says, but there are direct ways, sidetracks, wrong tracks, and dead-end tracks. Therefore endless relativity, in the sense that everybody can and will believe as she or he prefers, is not possible. But I also know that it is always possible to find better ways. There are no ways from which you cannot return, and, normally, there is not only one way that leads toward a given destination. Therefore theological dialogue, based on the model of truth as a way, has the character of sharing experiences, of questioning and counseling, of common searching, but rarely, if ever, the character of condemning.

The Functional Criterion:
Truth as an Event of Love

Our investigation of Matt. 16:18 has shown that the truth of new interpretations of the Bible cannot be decided according to a criterion of correspondence alone but that another criterion is necessary, a functional one. This criterion calls for the investigation of the effects of an interpretation in history and today. Our reflections about the biblical character of the criterion of correspondence have shown that this criterion cannot be handled in an objective manner, because it can never be detached from the way we use it, whether it be authoritarian and oppressive or communicative and dialogical. Let us turn therefore to this second functional criterion of truth. In my discussion of Matt. 16:18 I insisted that the fruits of a text in history must correspond to its intentions. Thus, with regard to Matthew, I asked whether the institution of the papacy corresponded to the ministry of the Matthean Peter, namely, to his proximity and fidelity to Jesus. But again it was evident that we have to widen this criterion and take into account the "canonical" level. Looking at the intended fruits of single texts can only be misleading. The "proper" fruits of 1 Cor. 14:34-35, for example, are that women should be silent in the church. But this fruit, according to the opinion of most people today, contradicts the fruits that are intended by the New Testament as a whole. This means that we must evaluate each single fruit of a biblical text in the light of what is the appropriate fruit of the entire New Testament.

This functional criterion corresponds philosophically to a pragmatic understanding of truth. Reception-critically, it questions not what an author said or intended, but what hearers or readers received. The importance of such a criterion is immediately evident when one considers the situation of a sermon. The professor of homiletics not only asks what you intended to say but also what people understood and how your sermon touched their lives. An excellent sermon is not "true" in the full sense of the word if nobody understood it or if it depressed people or made them passive. This is the kind of point Sigmund Freud made about the Christian commandment to love one's neighbor or one's enemy. Practically, he said, this commandment creates aggression toward the outside world because it is too high a demand and does not take into account naturally aggressive tendencies in the human psyche.[17] His point is well made. Biblical texts whose consequences have been hatred, exclusiveness, and injustice call for critical questioning, even if they correspond superficially to the history of Jesus or even if they are his own words.

I am thus pleading for a "hermeneutic of consequences," to use an expression of Dorothee Soelle.[18] For this kind of hermeneutic,

---

17. See U. Luz, *Matthew 1–7: A Continental Commentary*, trans. W. Linss (Minneapolis: Fortress Press, 1989) 349–50.
18. D. Soelle, *Phantasie und Gehorsam* (Stuttgart: Kreuz, 1968) 16.

the study of the history of effects is essential, because it shows what the consequences of biblical texts in history were. But what *is* its criterion? What are, to speak with Matthew, good fruit and bad fruit? Here again we cannot formulate fundamental values without a dialogue with the biblical and Christian tradition upon which we depend.

In the tradition of the Reformation, the difference between gospel and law was the most important functional criterion. The main difference between gospel and law lies not in their content but in their effect. The law terrifies and kills, but the gospel gives joy. Its word "makes everyone's heart laugh and rejoice and pours into every creature divine sweetness and comfort."[19] "True" in the theological sense is an attribute of the gospel; an interpretation of Scripture is "gospel" when it makes people free and happy and gives them life (cf. 2 Cor. 3:6). The Reformers formulated this criterion almost entirely on the level of receptivity and not on the level of human actions, because, for them, the word of God primarily was a gracious gift, and human actions always were something secondary, not constitutive, for the person. The history of effects of this Reformation criterion shows that it could not protect itself against the danger of becoming a merely private and a merely internal criterion. Especially our sisters and brothers from Third World countries have called our attention to the disastrous consequences of the separation of faith and praxis, person and acts, which was so influential in the Reformation tradition.

Therefore I would like to accentuate the Reformation criterion in a different way, a way that avoids the spiritualization and internalization of the "fruits" and includes deeds and life as well as the external, social dimensions of the biblical texts. Looking for such a criterion, I know that I am not neutral toward the biblical and ecclesiastical tradition. I make my choice, and I look for my formulation of the criterion. In my formulation I try to avoid the one-sidedness of our dominant Reformation tradition, and I try to answer the needs of our own current situation. I am convinced

---

19. M. Luther, "Predigten des 1526," in *M. Luthers Werke, Kritische Gesamtausgabe* (Weimar) 20.228f. See also *What Luther Says: An Anthology,* ed. E. M. Plass (St. Louis: Concordia, 1959) 2.739.

that there is no private or internal gospel and that the spiritual and the social dimension of the gospel must remain united. I try to think along the lines of Paul, for whom "faith" was "active in love" (Gal. 5:6). Naturally my formulation of the functional criterion also is open to dialogue and for revision.

I found the formulation of my "practical" criterion in Augustine's tractate on Christian doctrine. In this hermeneutical tractate he says, "Whoever . . . thinks that he understands the Holy Scriptures . . . but puts an interpretation upon them that does not tend to build up the twofold love of God and our neighbor does not yet understand them as he ought. If, on the other hand, someone draws a meaning from them that may be used for the building up of love, even though it does not disclose the precise meaning that the author . . . intended to express in that place—his error is not pernicious."[20] Elsewhere Augustine sets forth love as a criterion for figurative expressions, where ambiguities and arbitrary interpretations are particularly numerous, and he says that in evaluating figurative interpretations we have to ask whether an interpretation "tends to establish the reign of love."[21] If a literal interpretation builds up love, no allegorical interpretation is necessary.

Following Augustine I would formulate my criterion as follows: interpretations and applications of biblical texts are true insofar as they bring about love. For me, "love" has two dimensions. One is the love that I receive, namely, the love of God, promised through the texts and mediated through human beings. The other is the human love that I give to other people as my response to the love that was given to me. With this criterion, I want not to reject the internal dimension of the Reformation understanding of the gospel but to widen it. We have to ask whether an interpretation of a biblical text does indeed help others to experience joy, freedom, and identity, or whether it causes resignation or despair. But we also have to ask whether an interpretation helps others in their external needs, in their hunger and sufferings. We have to ask whether it helps to liberate them. Both sides belong to love.

My criterion is the result of a dialogue with the Bible. Augustine too took it from the Bible. It is clear that a functional criterion

20. *De doctrina Christiana* (trans. P. Schaff; NPNF I/2, 533) 1.36 (40).
21. Ibid., 3.15 (23) (ibid., 563).

cannot be formulated without recourse to tradition, and it cannot be formulated in an "impartial" way. Otherwise one simply would have to take the success of an interpretation in history as the criterion for its truth.[22] For me it is important that the criterion "love" is very close to the "ethical" Gospel of Matthew and his understanding of the will of God. In Matthew's interpretation of the parable of the four soils, only the fourth listener understands, and it is he who brings forth the fruits of the seed (13:23). In chapter 7 the Lord will judge his people according to their fruits and not according to theologically correct words or confessions (7:21-23). For Matthew, love is the criterion for truth and falseness of faith and also for real understanding.

But love is more than a Matthean criterion; it is a New Testament criterion. For John, "to remain in Christ" and "to remain in his love," or that "his words to remain in us" and that we "remain in his love" are closely related, if not identical (15:7-11). For Paul, "building up" (*oikodomē*) is the central criterion for the appropriateness of religious speech, and knowledge, which only puffs up, is contrasted with love, which builds up (1 Cor. 8:1; cf. chap. 14). Judging the Corinthian parties, Paul's criterion is not a theological one in the narrow sense, whereby his own theological position is better than another's. Paul's criterion is a functional one. Because the mere existence of parties makes the Corinthians behave like small children and destroys love and community in Corinth, the existence of parties in itself is not "true." I think that love is a central interpretation of the functional kernel of the history of Jesus, and, according to 1 John 4:16, is the very essence of God.

Let us pursue the meaning of love, as I understand it in the light of the Bible. First some negative statements. By "love" I do not mean merely to be nice to everybody. By "love" I also do not mean that you should first love yourself and other people only insofar as you love yourself. By "love" I do not mean the reasonable attitude that I can expect something only if I give something. But by "love" I mean this radical love without limits, about which Jesus spoke in the Sermon on the Mount. I mean a basically groundless

---

22. For example: 1 Cor. 14:34-36 would be "true" because this text was successful in keeping women silent in the churches for centuries!

affection, which New Testament texts testify to be the heavenly Father's attitude toward human beings. By love I mean a one-sided and partisan engagement for the cause of the poor, the outsiders, and the oppressed, which is central to Jesus' ministry. This is why the cry of the needy and oppressed is most important for the interpretation of love. By "love" I mean the limitless dedication to the human cause that finally led Jesus to his death in spite of the fact that he had opportunity to avoid this destiny. I do not want to claim a Christian monopoly on this love, but I want to say that, for me, Jesus is a model of this love, upon which I depend.

Love as a criterion of truth for the interpretation and application of biblical texts makes clear that there are no "true" interpretations of biblical texts in general, beyond concrete historical and social situations. It functions as a critical question mark to all separation of scholarly, historical, or dogmatic interpretation of biblical texts from the practical life of the interpreters. It is also a critical question mark for most of the churches, which define their identity or the identity of their gospel as doctrine beyond their praxis. It is a question mark for churches that believe that a common understanding of the gospel is possible without a common understanding of ethics or politics, or for churches that believe that only their proclamation and confession—but not their budgets—reveal the truth of their gospel.[23]

With this criterion I also find the possibility of formulating this crucial question about the office of Peter in the church. Does the office function as a real ministry, which helps to build up love for the sake of the unity of the church? I also find the possibility of questioning the Protestant definition of the church as a "mixed body" of good and bad people according to the parable of the tares. Does this definition function as an excuse for everything that is wrong in the church, or does it help to build up love?

The Convergence of the Two Criteria

The two criteria of truth—correspondence with the history of Jesus, and love—are not really two different criteria. They converge. The

---

23. This is important for European folk churches with their tax-based finance system!

history of Jesus, to which theological truth corresponds, is a history of uncompromising love. This is the final reason why the criterion of correspondence functioned more inclusively than exclusively. The history of Jesus functions as a model or example, not as a norm. It wants to provoke new, creative interpretations. This corresponds to love, which cannot be prescribed materially but has to be discovered anew in new situations. The history of Jesus functions as a dialogical criterion. Love is fundamentally dialogical.[24] Both criteria finally converge insofar as they both involve God deeply in the realm of humanity—in human history, the human experience of love.

The two criteria are not really different criteria but aspects of the same reality. For me, love is the most authentic form of the presence of the Spirit and of the presence of the risen Lord. For me, the criterion of love corresponds to the risen, present Lord, while the criterion of correspondence conforms to his human history. For me, the two criteria are expressions of the one Lord Jesus Christ. I understand my two criteria as a modern version of the classic unity of the human and the divine natures of Jesus. I understand them in analogy to the incarnation, which binds God to human history and points to the nonimposing, violable character of God's majesty. For me the two criteria are two sides of one sole christological criterion of truth.[25]

24. The Reformation is often criticized (especially from the side of Roman Catholics) because it has led to an extreme subjectivism in faith and to endless ecclesiastical splits. This is true. But against this implicit tendency of the Reformation understanding of the biblical message I would not like to establish an objective, suprahistorical truth (i.e., dogmas or decisions of a doctrinal ministry); I would like to root the personal interpretations in a process of communication and dialogue, which finally is constitutive for the church.

25. With this point I am not far away from what J. Panagopulos ("Christologie und Schriftauslegung beiden griechischen Kirchenvätern," *ZTK* 89 [1992] 41–58) describes as the christological interpretation of biblical texts in the hermeneutics of the Greek fathers: every text in its literal and spiritual interpretation is an expression of the living Christ and corresponds to his human and divine natures.

EPILOGUE

THE CHANGING INTERPRETATION OF THE BIBLE AND THE SITUATION IN EUROPE AND AMERICA TODAY

When I wrote these chapters and when I work on the Bible with my students and in my study, I naturally have the situation in Europe before my eyes. That is why I started this book with some remarks about my students, and that is why I return to the contextual character of this hermeneutical attempt now. Every interpretation of the Bible, every new significance of a biblical text in a new situation, is contextual; and, in the same way, every hermeneutic is contextual.

What is the situation of the Bible in Northern and Western Europe? Most people there never read the Bible and seldom go to church. With the flourishing life of all kinds of churches in the United States it is hard for Americans to imagine the extent to which Europe is a secularized and post-Christian world. The Bible is widely available but seldom read. It has become a book of minorities and a book of elitists.

Three different elitist minorities have to be mentioned. The first minority is what I would call the official church people: ministers, Christian educators, theologians, theology students, "professional laypeople." They use the Bible more or less for professional reasons, or they use the Bible as a legitimizing book for their institutions, their modes of behavior, or their beliefs.

The second minority includes the pietists, evangelical Christians, members of some Free churches, semifundamentalists, and fundamentalists. They use the Bible for their personal life and faith. Their basic tendency is to take the Bible as an authority that speaks directly and as a norm in their situations. They often practice a kind of "two-realm" life—private and public—not so much out of theological conviction but simply because the Bible, literally taken, does not say anything to modern social, political, economic, and technological life. Compared with the American situation, this minority is much smaller in most Protestant European countries.

The third minority that reads the Bible is what I call the modern "critical minorities,"[1] people who are unsatisfied with our materialistic, militaristic, egocentric, capitalistic, androcentric, and exploitative life-style. They are pacifists, feminists, active environmental activists, people engaged in Third World movements or in social work. They are not possessors of the truth but partners in a dialogue. They are sensitive to other people's suffering and to the global needs of our societies. In Europe they come partly from the first minority, partly from the second minority (not all the evangelicals are conservative!), and—the biggest part—from the secularized population. They read the Bible out of a feeling of desperation and helplessness. They look for alternatives and new directions. Many of them share a feeling of helplessness about the Bible. They perceive it to be a fascinating but ambiguous book and not easily applicable to their lives. Many of them are hesitant about the Bible, because for them the Bible traditionally stands for patriarchalism, "church," authority, doctrines, and rules. For many of them, the Bible is primarily a book of the past, full of dust, speaking from a different time and world.

That is how I see our situation. It is the third minority that I have in mind with my reflections and that is closest to my own heart and feeling. What do I hope to contribute to our European situation through my hermeneutics of the "history of effects" and of the "changing meaning" of the Bible? Six things:

1. I hope to help liberate Christians from premature pronouncements derived from the Bible about life, society, and church.

---

1. See K. Berger, *Hermeneutik des Neuen Testaments* (Gütersloh: G. Mohn, 1988) 76–78. For Berger the "critical minorities" are the primary applicants of the Bible he has in mind. For him (and for me) this includes the nucleus of ecclesiological hope.

I hope to show that the Bible does not want to function as a norm or as direct legitimator, but as a source of direction, ideas, and experiences. My hermeneutics have an antifundamentalist and anti-orthodox tendency.

2. I hope to contribute to encouraging Christian and non-Christian readers toward their own use of the Bible, their own listening, and their own applications and decisions. To interpret the Bible means that *we* recognize and take over our own responsibilities. I hope to strengthen the insight that no Christian values or truths can take away from us the responsibility for our own decisions, but rather to show that they help us to take over and accept our own responsibility. *We* have to decide how we obey, apply, modify, or change the call of the Bible in our situation. We cannot hide behind the Bible. Applications of biblical texts are always our own applications.

3. I hope to contribute toward a new interest in history and historical research. The study of history opens our eyes to the contextuality of truths, because it shows us something about the contextuality of other peoples' truths.[2] The study of history, while prohibiting us from taking historical truths as absolute, opens the possibility of using historical truths as models or examples.

4. I hope to help liberate the Bible from its isolation as a normative book of the past that has become meaningless for most people today. Many people think that the Bible is a normative book and then realize that as such it is useless, because it belongs to situations of the past that are very different from those of today. I think that the Bible, insofar as it is taken as a book of norms, has rightly become meaningless. But it becomes valuable when it is taken as a companion book, accompanying us on our own way and enabling and helping us in our situation to come to new insights out of old sources.

5. I hope to contribute to liberating the Bible from its function as a source book for abstract and general theological truths and doctrines. And I hope to contribute toward its functioning as a book of stories, examples, experiences, and thoughts that are fundamental for our own Christian experiences and life. I hope to help

2. There is a deep affinity between historical research and contextuality that is fundamental, for instance, for a theology of liberation.

show that the Bible is not simply a source for historical truths and eternal doctrines, but a resource for new life.[3]

6. I hope to contribute toward an open church that lives in dialogue because its members are aware of the contextuality of their own interpretations and do not claim to possess absolute truths. I hope to contribute toward a dialogue among various minorities who know that no undisputable and simple self-legitimation by means of the Bible is possible. I hope to contribute toward a dialogue in a church that knows that it cannot legitimate its own shape and actions *directly* by means of the Bible and therefore is capable of changing its institutions and actions according to the needs of love in the same way as the meaning of the Bible changes.

In these six points I see the contextual character of my hermeneutics in Europe.

But what about the United States? Most of the discussions I have had there were with students and colleagues coming from the so-called mainline churches. Among them there was a strong feeling about the unstable future of their churches, a concern about the growing secularization in their churches, about decreases in membership, and about diminishing cohesion. Among them there was also a feeling of unease toward the growing evangelical stream of American Christianity, which seems to meet—or to compensate for—the needs of an increasingly secularized society much better than do the mainline churches.

Many of my students had the impression that my approach could threaten the identity of mainline churches, because it seemed to strengthen exactly those tendencies toward relativism and ad libitum behavior that finally deprive the churches of their identity and dissolve them into the vacuous stream of American civil religion. "Are you a liberal?" was one of the questions I often heard—to my surprise! "The Presbyterian church stresses the diversity of its members anyway, sometimes to the destruction of their unity," a student said. Another student wrote, "Your comments about individual convictions that replace encompassing or eternal truths and the fact that each one believes as he or she desires as long as he or she does not condemn anyone else sound very much like

3. I owe the juxtaposition of "source" and "resource" to E. Schüssler Fiorenza.

American civil religion." Could it be that in the United States I am in the middle of a mainstream with my hermeneutics, namely, the mainstream toward religious pluralism, toward a religious modus operandi of "believe as you like as long as you don't disturb others"?

Every hermeneutic is contextual, and so is mine. Like the interpretations of biblical texts, biblical hermeneutics also has to be evaluated according to its correspondence with the Bible itself and according to the fruits it produces. Maybe my hermeneutic produces different fruits in Europe from what it does in the United States. Maybe it produces no fruits at all (this is the worst case); then it would have been a useless playing with ideas. I cannot defend my hermeneutics simply by saying that I am right. What I can do, and shall do now, is to make clear what I mean and what I do not mean, and thereby to protect my words against effects that I do not intend.

1. I do not want to deny that there is a truth that is beyond and above our personal identities. The word *God* indicates such a truth. Were I to deny this, then I would indeed privatize religion and reduce it to something akin to the idea that everybody needs "significance" for his or her life to make it meaningful. In this case the result would indeed be tolerance based on relativism. However, the word *God* includes the claim that this "significance" is more than what I decide or make it to be for myself; it claims that it encompasses me and is the basis of my life. There is a big difference between the absoluteness of the truth of God and the contextual and relative character of our interpretations of it! This difference leads to a continuous search for this absolute truth and to a continuous dialogue about it. For me, this search and dialogue are the middle between (1) the domination of some people by others in the name of *their* absolute truth and (2) the complete relativity of truth, as if truth were a matter of personal liking only.

For me, this process of dialogue is a basic characteristic of the church. Neither a total objectivization of truth, which leads to heteronomy, nor a complete subjectivization of truth, which corresponds to "civil religion," but the incarnation of the absolute truth in contextual situations is the way I seek. For me, both these extreme possibilities would destroy the identity of the church, but in different ways. In the first case, a church would become a heteronomous institution; in the second, a church would become a mere association of spiritually enlightened people who have friendly relations with each other but have little to say to one another.

2. I do not want to deny the necessity of a church. Quite the contrary! I understand Christ and his truth as a way we have to go and not as a position that we have to adopt or as a mere spirit of tolerance, that allows us not more than to be nice to one another. Therefore it is clear that only through our being on the way can Christ become real in our lives and in society. Being on the way is much more than to share (or to submit oneself to) some common doctrines or beliefs; it includes common experiences and common actions. Being on the way (not on many different ways, but on the way whose beginning and end is Christ! cf. John 14:6) includes community as a fundamental characteristic of a church, in opposition to exclusiveness and isolation.

3. Finally, if the meaning of the Bible changes, this does not lead churches toward dissolution but toward continuous reformation. "Being on the way" or "walking" is the fundamental characteristic of a church practicing discipleship, according to Matthew. The changing meaning of the Bible underscores the fact that the reformation of the church is never accomplished. The permanent reformation of the church, like the ongoing interpretation of the Bible and the creation of new moments of Christian identity in new situations, is a sign of a living church. Changing churches are not dying churches. Maybe this is true also for the American and the European mainline churches.

INDEX OF BIBLICAL REFERENCES

INDEX OF NAMES